DEATH
ON THE
NUECES

German Texans
Treue der Union

Rodman L. Underwood

EAKIN PRESS ⊕ Austin, Texas

Published in the United States of America
By Eakin Press
A Division of Sunbelt Media, Inc.
P.O. Drawer 90159 ☐ Austin, Texas 78709-0159
email: eakinpub@sig.net
☐ website: www.eakinpress.com ☐

2 3 4 5 6 7 8 9

1-57168-303-8

Library of Congress Cataloging-in-Publication Data

Underwood, Rodman L., 1930–
    Death on the Nueces / by Rodman L. Underwood.
        p.   cm.
    Includes bibliographical references and index.
    ISBN 1-57168-303-8
    1. Nueces River Affair, Tex., 1862. 2. German Americans—Texas—Texas
Hill Country—History—19th century. 3. Texas Hill Country (Tex.)—History—
19th century.   I. Title.
E473.4.U93   1999
973.7'32—dc21   99-17583
                                                                 CIP

CONTENTS

ACKNOWLEDGMENTS

An historian always has so many people to whom he is indebted. First, without the people who participated in the actual event, there is no history about which to write. We must always recognize their dedication and sacrifice. Second, the author must acknowledge all previous historians who have preceded him with their interpretations of the event. Any good writer researches these interpretations and builds upon this groundwork in developing his unique views and perceptions of the facts.

Nevertheless, while doing historical research, an author may come across an invaluable source. It seems trite to say that a book could not have been written without the assistance of another person. Nevertheless in this case it is true.

William Paul Burrier, Sr., of Leakey, Texas, knows more than any other living person about what happened before, during, and after the incident in August 1862 at the Nueces River. He is a thorough and tenacious researcher who has studied this matter for many years and has many source documents available. Furthermore, he is generous in sharing his knowledge with others, and enthusiastically and unselfishly does so.

While preparing this manuscript, Paul kept me straight on the facts; he encouraged me; he was my cheerleader! We talked on the phone for hours and he critiqued draft material. He helped me sort through the mass of data and recognize truth. I am indebted to him.

Rodman L. Underwood
Daytona Beach, Florida

v

PREFACE

One spring my wife and I were visiting friends in
Bandera, Texas. Joyce and Bob Storrs knew we were Civil
War buffs and invited us to take a drive to the town of
Comfort near San Antonio. They explained there was a
Civil War monument there, and we indicated interest in
seeing it. We supposed it to be a memorial to the
Confederate soldiers who had died in that conflict since
we had seen many such memorials in towns throughout
the south. Additionally, I had been a student of the
American Civil War for a quarter century and thought I
was quite well schooled. However, I was unaware of what
was missing in these small German towns in the Texas
Hill Country. None of the town centers displayed a statue
of the Confederate rifleman that was so common in other
southern towns. What was to follow would remind me of
the quotation attributed to Harry S. Truman: "The only
thing new in this world is the history you don't know."

We found the monument without difficulty but to our
surprise it memorialized the Union dead, not the
Confederate dead; civilians, not soldiers; and Germans,
not Anglos. The monument contained only names, and
adjacent to it was a sketchy plaque indicating why the
monument was there. We learned its name was the *Treue
der Union* (Loyalty to the Union) monument and that it
was constructed in 1866 over the common grave of thirty-
six area pioneers who had died in the 1862 Nueces River
massacre while fleeing to Mexico.

I was ignorant of the fact that this part of Texas had
been populated by many Germans, that there was such a

place as the Nueces River, and that there had been a massacre. My ignorance served the purpose of stimulating my curiosity and sent me on this quest for knowledge.

What intrigued me most was the hate that men must have held to commit this massacre. James A. Michener states in *Texas* that these people had been killed " . . . in one of the least justified actions of the war" (754). I knew from my study of Civil War history that these had been violent times with brother killing brother in battle, and with individual citizens killing one another over their stance in the war. However, I was not aware of any other incident where a group of civilians, seeking safety outside the United States because of their opposition to slavery, had been tracked and hunted down by a military organization for over 100 miles, and then was ambushed and killed. I knew that slavery was a passionate issue for which men were dying on the battlefield. It seemed to me, however, that there was more than mere passion at work here. I thought there must be a whole lot of hate that accounted for seething feelings erupting into murder. What was the justification for this action?

I hold a strong dislike for hate and negative feelings toward my fellow man. Usually ignorance and prejudice trigger these feelings. I am driven to understand their roots so that I might contribute something toward diminishing their potency. Consequently, I was persuaded to attempt an analysis of the factors underlying the Nueces River Massacre. I set out on my quest, and this is the result.

While engaging in a study such as this, one invariably is changed by the facts he accumulates. An historical event is never as simple as it may seem. Because of what I had read on the monument, I began my exploration with a bias against the South and the Confederacy—against those people who murdered innocent German civilians. As my study progressed I moved toward more understanding of, and appreciation for, the stance of both sides and became saddened by this human tragedy. I uncovered multiple layers of facts and different interpretations of those facts. I ran across misstatements, misunderstandings, conflicting evidence, prejudice, bias, lies, and other such detritus through which the researcher must sift. There is a paucity of documents dealing with the Anglo Texan and Confederate perception of the issues, and an abundance of documents from German sources that are emotionally charged accounts and recollections of the Nueces River massacre. I have attempted to balance the contrasting views as best I could while trying to recognize and control my own biases. Nevertheless, there were gaps left, which I filled as intelligently as possible based upon my understanding of the various cultures involved, and of the broad American Civil War picture. I hope my analyses of the factors underlying this event give the reader increased sensitivity to the hate and other negative emotions he sees around him today, so that he may become a force in neutralizing them.

Throughout this narrative I refer to the Texas Hill Country. This is a beautiful section of Central Texas with gently rolling hills that must have reminded the German settlers of their homeland. This country is located northwest of San Antonio and west of Austin, and I concentrate upon three coterminous counties: Kendall, Kerr, and Gillespie. This area is along Interstate 10 as it meanders northwest and is a triangular section of land with the community of Boerne representing the apex and the towns of Kerrville and Fredericksburg constituting the base. The small town of Comfort is in the center.

A few years before the Civil War, Frederick Law Olmsted took a trip through Texas and wrote about it in *A Journey Through Texas*. He tells of crossing the Colorado River and entering the Hill Country where he finds that live-oak trees, that are characteristic of this section, gradually give way to dwarf mesquite to the west of San Antonio. He was awed by the country and says, "The live-oaks are often short, and even stunted in growth, lacking the rich vigor and full foliage of those further east . . . . As far west as beyond the Guadalupe, they are thickly hung with the gray Spanish moss, whose weird color, and slow, pendulous motions, harmonize peculiarly with the tone of the tree itself, especially where, upon the round, rocky, mountain ledges, its distorted roots cling, disputing a scant nourishment with the stunted grass" (130).

The Nueces River is referred to throughout this book. Early Spanish explorers, who found either pecan or pin-ion nuts in the vicinity, discovered this river. *Nueces* means "nut" in Spanish. The site of the Nueces River affair is in Kinney County near Del Rio.

TIMELINE

1820s	Germans begin settling in Texas.
1823	Austin is founded.
1835-1836	Texas secedes from Mexico and the Republic of Texas is proclaimed.
1841	Texas grants land contracts to agents of immigrants.
1842	*Adelsverein* is organized. Henri Castro establishes a colony near San Antonio.
1842-1843	Republic of Texas and Mexico engage in land disputes.
1845	Texas is annexed by the United States and becomes the 28th state on December 29. Germans settle in the Hill Country in Central Texas and New Braunfels is founded.
1846-1847	United States and Mexico engage in war. Meusebach's treaty is signed with the Comanches in the Hill Country. "The Forty" settle a commune at Bettina.
1848	The Treaty of Guadalupe-Hidalgo is signed, ending Mexican claims to Texas and other territory. "The Forty-Eighters" settle at Sisterdale.
1854	Ernst Altgelt organizes Comfort.
1860	Abraham Lincoln is elected president.

March 1861	Texas secedes from the Union and joins the Confederate States of America.
April 1861	Fort Sumter is fired upon and the Civil War commences.
June 1861	The Union Loyal League is formed.
March 1862	The Union Loyal League Militia is formed.
May 1862	Martial law is declared in Texas.
July 1862	Captain Duff is ordered to put down rebellion in the Hill Country.
August 1862	The initial Nueces River affair occurs.
August 1866	The *Treue der Union* Monument is dedicated.
August 1996	The Second *Treue der Union* Monument is rededicated.

PART ONE

THE
GATHERING

CHAPTER 1.

TWO GUARDS

T he cheerful group of young men sat around the campfire on this hot August evening in Texas feasting on game they had shot and honey they had gathered during their trip. They enjoyed one another's company as they sang German songs and made patriotic speeches about the glory of America and its Constitution, and the freedoms and opportunities afforded them.

They had left their loved ones in Central Texas a week earlier to ride their horses to Mexico. They disliked leaving their families, but they hated even more being drafted into an alien army and being forced to fight against their adopted country. Most of them had arrived in the United States of America within the past fifteen years. They loved America and were determined to be forever loyal to her.

Now they found themselves in the midst of a Civil War and living in a state which had seceded from the Union. Worse, they were considered politically incorrect because they believed in the equality of man and preservation of the Union. They took seriously their oath of loyalty to their adopted country. Other Texans had gone to war to preserve slavery and to form a new alliance of southern states that they named the "Confederate States of America." Those forming the new Confederation were in the majority. They insisted that the minority Germans conform by signing a loyalty oath to the Confederacy and by being drafted into the Confederate army. The Germans would not do this because their loyalty was with the Union.

The Germans had been repressed and intimidated for their minority views for the past year. Because they could not be disloyal to the Union, they decided to flee over 100 miles to neutral Mexico, where other Germans had fled earlier. Many of them hoped that, once in Mexico, they would be able to journey to a Gulf of Mexico port and board a ship bound for New Orleans. There they would join the Union army and fight for their beliefs.

Two members of the armed group were Leopold Bauer and Ernst Beseler. Bauer was from the vicinity of Comfort, Texas, in Kendall County. He was twenty-three years of age, having been born in Prussia in 1839. He arrived in the Comfort area in 1854. He and Beseler had been acquainted for some time because they lived near each other. Beseler was born around 1842 in Wesel, Germany, and was twenty years old. He arrived in Texas in 1848. Both men were members of the Kendall County Company of the Hill Country Militia.

The group was encamped near the west branch of the Nueces River in Kinney County on this hot Saturday evening, August 9, 1862. The clearing they had chosen exposed them to a southerly breeze. It still was around seventy-five degrees, but this was a relief from the oppressive ninety-five-degree heat earlier in the day. There would be no rain to cool the night. The summer of 1862 was a severe drought season, but the river water was clear, cool, and abundant for the men and their mounts. With full bellies, most of the men had gone to sleep near moonset at around 11:00 P.M., while Bauer and Beseler were posted nearby to guard duty. Meanwhile the hobbled horses dined on the thick tufts and patches of nutritious and palatable short grass. Life was good for man and beast.

The hours passed into Sunday morning. At about 3:00 A.M. Bauer thought he heard horses and men nearby and went to investigate. He stumbled into a group of men on the move and they shot him dead. Beseler went to investigate and encountered a hail of gunfire from Sharps rifles. He was the second to die. The men in camp were alarmed and began firing into the dark.

Local historian Paul Burrier studying his maps on August 2, 1998. The photograph was taken on or near the site where the Unionists assembled for their trip to Mexico around this same date in 1862. Paul is a descendant of the leader of the Unionist group, Maj. Fritz Tegener.   —Author's private collection

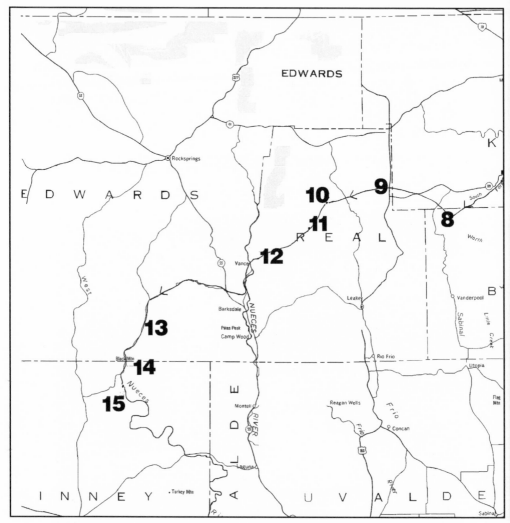

This map contains points at which Confederate and Union forces were located on specific days. The text follows the map points and generally is in chronological order for each group. They departed from different locations on different days but collided with one another on the West Prong of the Nueces River on the morning of August 10, 1862. It is noted that some dates may not coincide with dates found elsewhere in the book. This arises because primary source material uses different dates for days of departure (in some accounts memory has faded over time and in other accounts people define departure differently). Some dates simply are not known with certainty and are the subject of ongoing research.

—Researched and produced by Paul Burrier

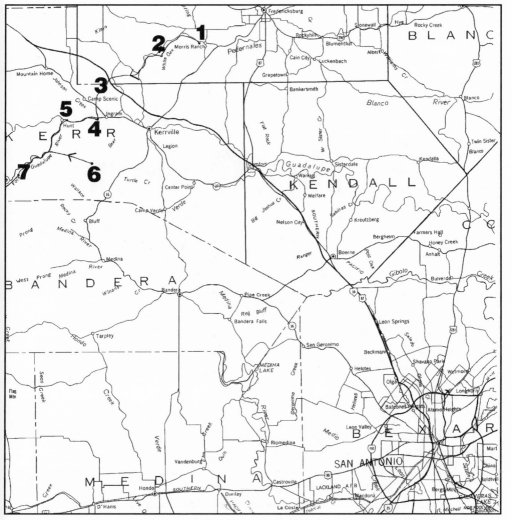

1. *Camp Pedernales*—Location of Duff's and Donelson's Companies and detachments of Taylor's 8th Battalion Texas Cavalry.

2. *Camp Davis*—Location of Davis' Company F, The Frontier Regiment. Confederates departed midday August 4.

3. *Henderson Farm*—Most likely Sebird Henderson's farm where Confederates spent night of August 4.

4. *Guadalupe River*—Point on Guadalupe River where Confederate pursuit force reached the river. From here they turned west.

5. *Tegener Creek*—Where Confederates spent night of August 5.

6. *Union Assembly Area on Turtle Creek*—Where Unionists met in preparation for trip to Mexico, and where they received supplies from supporters. Likely location where Charles Burgmann had supplies taken from him. Unionists departed August 3.

7. *Main Unionist Camp*—Near headwaters of South Fork of Guadalupe River. Where Unionists spent night of August 3. Where Confederates spent night of August 6.

8. *Head of North Prong of Medina River*—Where Unionists spent night of August 4. Confederates reached on morning of August 7.

9. *Headwater of West Prong of Frio River*—Where Unionists spent night of August 5. Confederates reached on afternoon of August 7.

10. *Point on high plateau*—Where Confederates spent night of August 7, a "dry camp."

11. *Head of Bullhead Creek*—Where Unionists spent night of August 6. Confederates reached about 10 A.M. August 8.

12. *Where Bullhead Creek meets East Prong Nueces River*—Where Unionists spent night of August 7 and where four Texan Anglos joined them. Confederates reaches around 2 P.M. on August 8.

13. *Point "high in mountains"*—Where Confederates spent night of August 8, a "dry camp."

14. *Point "deep in mountains"*—Where Unionists spent night of August 8, a "dry camp." Confederates reached about midday August 9.

15. *West Prong Nueces River*. Battle Site—Unionists reached about mid-morning on August 9 and made camp. Confederate scouts reached area in mid-afternoon.

CHAPTER 2

THE HILL COUNTRY MILITIA

T he men in the camp on the Nueces River were members of the Hill Country Militia, which was the military arm of the Hill Country Union Loyal League. On August 1, 1862, they had gathered at Turtle Creek, which is located eight miles south of Kerrville, Texas, in Kerr County to the northwest of San Antonio. They were responding to the call of Fritz Tegener. He had been tentatively selected as the leader of the Militia on March 24, 1862, at a preliminary organizational meeting. A formal election of leaders took place in early May 1862 at a secret assembly of the men in the mountains between Comfort and Fredericksburg where Bear Creek originates. Three companies were formed and they were: the Gillespie County Company (the major town is Fredericksburg), the Kendall County Company (composed of men from the small towns of Comfort, Sisterdale, and Boerne), and the Kerr County Company (the major town is Kerrville). The elected leaders of each company were as follows: Gillespie County Company, Jacob Kuechler, Captain, Valentine Hohmann, Lieutenant; Kendall County Company, Ernest Cramer, Captain, Hugo Degener, Lieutenant; and Kerr County Company, Henry Hartman, Captain, Phil G. Temple, Lieutenant. In addition, an advisory board was formed and Eduard Degener, the head of the Union Loyal League, was named chairman.

The members of the Gillespie and Kendall county units were predominantly of Germanic origin, while the Kerr County group was predominantly American-born Union supporters. Sometimes the Kerr County company was referred to as the American Company to distinguish it from the other two groups. The three companies were formed into a battalion under the command of Major Fritz Tegener.

Fritz Tegener, age twenty-nine, had been born in 1833 in Prussia. He immigrated to Texas with his brothers Gustav and William, and arrived in Kerr County about 1856. On December 21, 1858, he married sixteen-year-old Susan Elizabeth Benson, who was a native of Illinois. They lived in Kerr County and had one child, Texana. Fritz made a living first as a carpenter and later as a miller. In 1860 those living in his household included his wife and child, his brother Gustav, and his wife's brother, Thomas Benson.

On July 20, 1862, Fritz Tegener was at work in his gristmill when he became aware that the Hill Country had been declared to be in rebellion against the Confederate States of America. He conferred with Eduard Degener about leading militia members to Mexico, where they might join the Union army.

On July 25, 1862, Eduard Degener came to the home of John W. Sansom on Curry's Creek and told him about the organization of the Hill Country Militia. He advised Sansom that Major Tegener would be leading elements of the militia to Mexico. He invited Sansom to join the group as a guide because of his knowledge of the Edwards Plateau and of suitable crossings across the Rio Grande. Sansom agreed to join them, settled his home affairs, and went to the meeting place around August 1.

Also on July 25 Major Tegener had informed his people that anyone who wished to leave Texas and flee to Mexico should assemble on August 1. The announced plan was to travel by horse and pack train out of Texas to

Matamoros, Mexico, where those who wished could board a ship for New Orleans, Louisiana. Once there they could join a Union cavalry group that was being formed.

The planned route was south and west of San Antonio so as to avoid settlements, Confederate strongholds, and other populous areas in order to avoid detection. They were to travel across the wilderness of the Edwards Plateau, crossing the Medina, Frio, and Nueces rivers. They hoped to cross the Rio Grande into Mexico, where the Devils River enters the larger river and provides a suitable ford. This is near the present town of Del Rio, Texas.

The journey would be a strenuous one. The topography of the Hill Country in Central Texas is hilly and there are occasional small canyons coupled with freshwater springs, rivers, and streams. The soils of the surrounding Edwards Plateau are rocky, shallow, and covered with a layer of limestone. Average annual rainfall is around twenty-five inches with most of it occurring in the spring and fall.

The summers are hot; drought conditions may exist then. Trees include white shinoak, live-oak, Texas oak, and ashe juniper. The latter tree is often referred to as cedar-brake. Common grasses include curly mesquite, buffalograss, and Texas wintergrass. Spring wildflower displays can be spectacular if the weather conditions and rainfall cooperate. Common flowers are the bluebonnet, the knotweed leafflower, and the velvet bundleflower. Game is plentiful and consists of white-tailed deer, Rio Grande turkey, armadillo, and jackrabbits. Bird life is abundant and consists of mourning doves, bobwhite quail, the black-capped vireo, and the golden-cheeked warbler. This is hard, barren country in which to travel. The land, especially southward from the Nueces River toward Mexico, begins to assume desert-like characteristics. In August the days are scorchers, the heat is still oppressive at night, there is little rainfall, small streambeds dry up, and underfoot are snakes, scorpions, and other such varmints.

Sixty-four men—all of them under thirty-five years of

age and all but two of them Germans—elected to join Major Tegener on this hazardous, nearly 150-mile, journey. An experienced Indian and bandit fighter signed on to guide them through this sparsely settled and inhospitable country. His name was John William Sansom, and he was one of the few non-Germans in the group.

Most of the older German Unionists chose not to subject themselves to this strenuous trip over the rough terrain. They believed they were needed to carry on the basic tasks of their communities, such as farming, commerce, transport, and lumbering. Also they felt an obligation to look after the women and children of the departing Unionists.

The Hill Country Militia departed from their Turtle Creek assembly point on August 2, 1862. The next day Confederate Lt. Colin D. McRae left his camp.

During a drought in August 1998, the dry creek bed of the Nueces looking upstream. (County Road 334 is crossing the river.)
—Author's private collection

CHAPTER 3.

SECESSION

I n 1859 secession was discussed in Texas but was not the central concern of most people. Circumstances were about to change their views. These circumstances revolved around the matter of dealing with hostile Indians, a cotton economy in East Texas tied to slavery, the rise of the national Republican Party and abolitionists, and the increasing pressure toward secession after the election of Abraham Lincoln.

The first problem—that of dealing with hostile Indians who had killed many Texans through the 1850s—was exacerbated by the perception of many Texas citizens that the Federal government failed to adequately protect the frontiersmen from Indian attack. Partially in response to this need for protection, the Texas Rangers were formed. The state then billed the Federal government for the expenses of the Rangers, but Congress found various reasons to drag its feet on this matter (Buenger 17). Texans resented the Federal government's inaction and inadequate response to the Indian problem. The citizens of the state lost faith in the national government and became disposed to the notion of secession from the Union.

A second factor was the well-developed cotton economy in East Texas that was tied to slavery and the plantation system. King Cotton had flourished in the lower South and had expanded especially from the states of Mississippi and Alabama into East Texas, where the soil and climate were conducive to a profitable crop. Cotton was a labor-intensive crop and slavery was tied to it because cheap labor helped to ensure profit. Thus there was a desire to maintain that "peculiar institution."

The third development bringing pressure to bear upon Texas was the inception of the Republican Party. As far back as 1830, sectional lines had been hardening on the slavery question. Southerners favored the expansion of slavery into new territories because cotton rapidly exhausted the soil and consequently new fertile lands were required. Northern abolitionists favored the immediate end to slavery on moral grounds. With the conclusion of the Mexican War, the addition of new territories to the United States renewed pressure for the expansion of slavery to the north and west.

The Compromise of 1850 relieved tension over slavery for a time. It provided that California would be admitted as a slavery-prohibited state, that New Mexico and Utah would be organized without mention of slavery, that claims of Texas to a portion of New Mexico would be satisfied by a payment of $10 million, and that a "Fugitive Slave Law" would be enacted to enable catching runaway slaves and returning them to their masters.

Senator Stephen A. Douglas rekindled the fire on the slavery issue in 1854, when he introduced the Kansas-Nebraska Bill. This legislation would supersede the limits on slavery territory enacted through the Missouri Compromise of 1820 by allowing settlers to carry slaves into two territories (Kansas and Nebraska) and allowing the inhabitants to determine whether those territories should enter the Union as slave or free states. The bill became law and as a result the Whig Party, which straddled the fence on the expansion of slavery, was doomed. In its place a powerful, new force rose, the Republican Party. The Republican Party demanded that slavery be excluded from all the new territories. It quickly grew, and one year later an Illinois politician, Abraham Lincoln, joined the party. He frequently spoke of his moral opposition to slavery and of his belief that the national government had a right to exclude the expansion of slavery. This stance was echoed in the Republican platform, and the abolitionists in the North became an increasingly potent force. In response, the Democratic Party attacked and branded the other party as "Black Republicans" because allegedly they would disturb slavery and race relations and would menace white supremacy. In fact the "Black Republicans" did support abolition of slavery and voting rights for blacks. That party opposed the Fugitive Slave Law of 1850, which authorized slave owners to cross state lines to recapture their property (runaway slaves). When the law withstood legal challenges, the Republicans supported state personal liberty laws, which prohibited the use of state facilities to recapture runaway slaves, and this made the law difficult to enforce.

The Supreme Court's infamous Dred Scott decision in 1857 brought the nation closer to upheaval. Scott was a Missouri slave who had been taken by his master to live in territory that excluded slavery through the terms of the Northwest Ordinance. Master and slave returned to Missouri, where Scott sued for his freedom on the basis of his previous residence in free territory. The court ruled against him and stated he was not a citizen, that slaveholders had the right to take their property anywhere they pleased, and that Congress could not restrict the expansion of slavery. The importance of the court's decision was that it invalidated compromises on slavery that had been crafted by Congress for years. Thus the battle lines were drawn.

Finally, Lincoln was elected president in 1860 and took office in March 1861. With his election there was alarm throughout the South that the new president would interfere with the right of a state to maintain the institution of slavery. Secession, as an option, had been discussed for at least the last decade, and it gained impetus throughout the South when Lincoln was elected. States in the lower South reacted first. South Carolina seceded in December 1860 and was followed by other Southern states in January 1861. On February 4, 1861, the Confederate States of America (CSA) was founded and the die was cast for Texas.

Texans were divided on the issue of secession. Secession sentiment was strongest in East Texas, where the economy was tied to slavery. That part of Texas was predominantly populated with Anglos from the lower South (Georgia, Alabama, and Mississippi), where plantation society was a way of life. These folks comprised the largest cultural group in the state (Buenger 12). Union sentiment was strongest among Germans in Central Texas and Anglos along the Red River who had migrated from the upper South, especially from the states of Tennessee and Kentucky. Unionism was based on the belief that the Union was of great value because it satisfied a longing to bind different people together toward a common goal. The Constitution was revered.

Texas moved toward secession in February 1861. Secessionists were well organized, while those in opposition tended to be less well organized and remained silent. One author asserts that one-third of Texans actively supported the Confederacy, one-third remained neutral, and one-third supported the Union (Elliott 83). Secessionists tended to "bulldoze" their way toward approval of secesion; an important organization providing secessionist leadership was the Knights of the Golden Circle (KGC). This group had been at the forefront of the secession movement since the late 1850s.

The secessionists used force to seize Federal government property in Texas before the statewide referendum on secession took place. Texas negotiated with Brig. Gen. David E. Twiggs, U.S. Commander for the Department of Texas, for surrender of all Federal property in Texas. The negotiations broke down, and in early February 1861 Twiggs and his 160 men in San Antonio were confronted by armed troops consisting of 1,100 state troops and 150 KGC troops (OR Ser. 1, Vol. 53, 628-29). Twiggs surrendered the Federal property five days before the referendum on the ordinance of secession took place (Heidler 39-41). The referendum to secede passed by a three-to-one margin (46,129 to 14,697) on February 23, 1861, and Texas joined the CSA on March 2, 1861.

An indication of secession divisiveness in Texas was that Governor Sam Houston would not support the decision of the majority of the voters to secede. He was removed from office and the lieutenant governor served out his term. Besides Governor Houston, there were other important leaders who opposed secession, such as a former governor, congressmen, and state legislators. Particularly in some German counties, opposition to secession was marked. For example, in Fredericksburg and Gillespie County, which was seventy-five percent German, the vote was 398-to-16 against secession. Most of the Germans who had settled in the Hill Country supported Governor Houston's opposition to secession because they abhorred the idea of one man owning another man. Some of them later openly expressed their loyalty to the Union by refusing to sign an oath of allegiance to the Confederacy, and they were branded as traitors. When a majority feels threatened by a rebellious minority, the response frequently is repression by the majority, usually in the form of intimidation by threat of property destruction or even threat of death. This occurred in Central Texas and set the stage for the later events at the Nueces River.

The land between the Rio Grande and the Nueces River is rich in the history of armed conflict and violence arising from disputed land ownership. This history serves as a backdrop for what was to happen in the Nueces River affair. Especially during 1842 and 1843 there were frequent armed conflicts between Mexicans and Texans. At one point San Antonio was seized by Mexicans, and the Texans launched a retaliatory raid into Mexico. After Texas was admitted to the Union in 1845, Mexico broke off diplomatic relations with the United States because of the dispute between the two countries as to the ownership of the land between these two important rivers. Mexico claimed the U.S. boundary extended only to the Nueces River to the north, while the United States claimed the U.S. boundary extended to the Rio Grande to the south. This land dispute would lead to war.

After Mexico had terminated diplomatic relations, the

United States responded by positioning an "Army of Observation" under the command of Gen. Zachary Taylor on the Nueces River. President Polk subsequently moved that army to the Rio Grande. On April 24, 1846, Mexican troops attacked and President Polk declared a state of war. Many in Congress opposed the war because they saw this as a device to enable the South to expand slavery into the southwest. Nevertheless the war commenced and Mexico was defeated. Mexico lost what today is California, New Mexico, Nevada, Utah, most of Arizona, and parts of Colorado and Wyoming. The 1848 Treaty of Guadalupe-Hidalgo also established the Texas-Mexico boundary at the Rio Grande. The fragile balance of power between the pro-slavery and anti-slavery forces was becoming unhinged, and this indirectly led to the Civil War.

In spite of the 1848 treaty, the land between these two great rivers remained in dispute, and many Mexicans living north of the Rio Grande felt their land was being illegally expropriated from them by the U.S. judicial system. In response to this perceived injustice, the Mexican folk hero Gen. Juan Cortina attacked Brownsville, Texas, in 1859. This launched the "First Cortina War" and Mexicans hoped their leader would drive the Americans back to the Nueces River. United States soldiers were called in to put down the rebellion, and General Cortina was driven back into Mexico. The commander of the U.S. Military Department of Texas, Col. Robert E. Lee, warned Mexican officials that their "bandits" would not be allowed to raid Texas along the north side of the Rio Grande from bases in Mexico.

The Civil War commenced on April 12, 1861, with the firing on Fort Sumter at Charleston, South Carolina. Two days before the firing upon Fort Sumter, there was a revolt against the Confederate authorities at Carrizo, Texas, which is near the Nueces River battle site. Armed Mexican Union sympathizers threatened to hang county officials to prevent them from taking the oath of allegiance to the Confederacy. They were dissuaded but on April 15, 1861, a Confederate company under the command of

Capt. Matthew Nolan surrounded these dissidents at the nearby Clareno Ranch. The dissidents were ordered to surrender, a firefight ensued, and Nolan later bragged that "nine Black Republicans" (supporters of the Republican Party and Abraham Lincoln) had been killed (Sanchez n.p.). This was the beginning of the so-called "Second Cortina War," which was more of a pro-Cortina, anti-Texas action than a Union-Confederate battle.

In response to this skirmish, General Cortina crossed the Rio Grande near Carrizo, where he gathered about 1,500 men on May 19, 1861, to engage a Confederate force that defeated him. Again he was driven into Mexico but there arose a concerted guerrilla movement led by Octaviano Zapata. The "Zapatistas," as they were known, were encouraged by Union agents and they attacked Confederate supply trains and generally caused mischief for the Confederates. There were hangings, killings of noncombatants, and property destruction by both sides. Skirmishes continued through 1861 and 1862, and the Confederates had to devote considerable effort to suppress the "Zapatistas."

Throughout 1862 Union agents were active in Mexico, a neutral nation, agitating and encouraging dissidents fleeing Texas to join the United States Army. In particular they were active around Matamoros, Mexico, across the Rio Grande from Brownsville, Texas. German Texans who had fled to Mexico often took a boat (which had been arranged by the U.S. Consul) from Matamoros to New Orleans, where they could enlist in the First Texas Cavalry (Union). This unit was formed on October 26, 1862, by former South Texas district judge Edmund Jackson Davis. Also, Brownsville was an important port that was subject to Union blockade because it was from here that Texas cotton was being shipped to Europe and England in exchange for guns and supplies.[1] The Confederacy was interested in controlling the Rio Grande border to prevent Texans from fleeing to Mexico and to keep cotton flowing to Europe and England.

This ongoing guerrilla activity, skirmishes in the

"no-man's" land south of the Nueces River, and efforts by the Confederacy to control the Rio Grande border with Mexico, all served as a backdrop to the incident which was to occur on the Nueces in August 1862. The Germans, as we shall see, fled into a volatile mixture of power, fear, anger, and retribution. The stage was set for a disaster.

Violence elsewhere helped to fan the flames of passion. The nearby state of Missouri was even more divided than Texas. Admiration for the Union existed side by side with devotion to the Confederacy. A flash point was St. Louis, where there were thousands of German immigrants who had little use for slavery. The U.S. arsenal there was a prize coveted by Confederate sympathizers who made preliminary moves to capture the weapons housed therein. The pro-South governor activated the state militia to take the arsenal. The Union reacted by sending Federal troops on a preemptory strike upon the state militia camp on May 10, 1861. The state militia surrendered without a shot. Southern prisoners were marched back toward the arsenal by recently activated German soldiers. The Germans received invectives and threats from the crowd of Southern sympathizers watching the affair. The crowd menaced the Germans with revolvers, and the situation soon boiled over into violence. General firing ensued on both sides, resulting in casualties among both soldiers and civilians. Rioting continued the next day, and again the German regiment was in the middle of a firefight. Thirty-six people died during those two days.

This incident, which undoubtedly was reported in Texas, displayed the deep hatred and mistrust of Germans as well as the fury connected with the Union-Confederacy rift. Two young soldiers reflect the depth of acrimony. One, a German, John T. Buegel, 3rd Missouri Volunteer Infantry, wrote, "When the haughty young Americans [Southern supporters] were taken into custody by the second regiment, composed of Germans, and as prisoners were marched to the arsenal, their rage knew no bounds. But to no avail. They simply were prisoners, and the Dutch, as we were generally called, were masters of the situation" (Catton 499, note 13). A Southern soldier wrote, "My blood boils in my veins when I think of the position of Missouri—held in the Union at the point of Dutchmen's bayonets. I feel outraged—you may imagine how hard it is for men to endure it" (Catton 499, note 13).

Soon after this the Civil War began to swirl around Texas and blood began to flow freely. Five months before the incident at the Nueces River, heavy battles occurred near Texas. On March 7-8, 1862, there was the Battle of Pea Ridge, Arkansas. This battle arose from Federal efforts to secure control of Missouri. The Union victory there ended any serious Confederate threat to Missouri. Several weeks later, on March 26-28, Texas troops fought the Battle of Glorieta, New Mexico. These troops were intent on taking a Federal supply center 100 miles northeast of Santa Fe, New Mexico, but they were repulsed. Two weeks later, on April 6-7, 1862, the massive Battle of Shiloh took place at Pittsburgh Landing on the Tennessee River. A Texan, Gen. Albert Sidney Johnston, led the Confederate Army, which consisted of many Texas troops. He had been a soldier and secretary of war for the Republic of Texas and had fought in the Mexican War. Gen. Ulysses S. Grant opposed him at Shiloh, and the battle was fought by the South with the hope of destroying Grant's army before help could arrive. The Union forces drove the Confederate forces from the field and as a result maintained control over the Tennessee and Cumberland rivers. General Johnston was killed in the action, and Texas mourned for a great soldier. Shiloh had launched this nation into protracted warfare, and the Lone Star State was propelled into the midst of the Civil War.

During the spring of 1862 small groups of Germans in the Hill Country discussed the increasing tension over the past year or so between themselves and Texans who were on the other side of the issues which had sparked a civil war. These Germans were loyal to the Union and were opposed to slavery. The other Texans were loyal to the Confederacy and were in favor of slavery. Passions ran high. The two sides were polarized.

Since the election of Abraham Lincoln in 1860 there had been serious talk of secession. In a vote held on February 23, 1861, the citizens of Texas decided to withdraw from the Union by a vote of 46,128 to 14,697, but eighteen counties out of 152 voted to remain in the Union. The majority of these eighteen counties were in the Hill Country, where Germans were the dominant group. For example, Comfort and Fredericksburg voted by large margins to remain in the Union. Texas was divided on the slavery issue, as were other states in the Confederacy and the Union. Households were divided on the issue as well. Nevertheless, Texas joined the Confederate States of America on March 2, 1861, and a month later the Civil War began.

In June 1861 eighteen German men from the Hill Country formed the Union Loyal League, the purpose of which was to remain loyal to the United States of America. In time the organization grew to about 500 men and about two-thirds of the League members were Germans while one-third were Anglos (Ransleben 103-115). Germans held the leadership positions. The Hill Country Union Loyal League was part of a state organization whose goal was to restore the Federal government in Texas. It was primarily a political organization that initially hoped to accomplish its goal by peaceful means such as speech-making and persuasion. Later efforts were directed toward devaluation of Confederate currency and opposition to drafting men into the Confederate army. The local League was loosely affiliated with a larger national organization variously known as the Union League or the Loyal League. This organization had been initiated in the North by business and professional men for the purpose of supporting Abraham Lincoln and preserving the Union. In effect it was an auxiliary of the Republican Party.

Throughout much of 1861 the organization in the Hill Country was tolerated without reprisal by the secessionists because it engaged in little hostile action against the Confederacy. Similar leagues were found elsewhere in Texas. In Gainesville, near the Oklahoma border, a Loyal League was formed about the same time as in the Hill

Country. In addition there was an active organization in San Antonio, and nearby Austin was a hotbed of Unionist activity throughout the war. In all of these Loyal Leagues there were isolated threats of active revolution against the Confederacy, but these threats simmered to passive resistance. There were instances of guerrilla-like activity by lawless groups known as "bushwhackers."

Predating the Union Loyal League was the Knights of the Golden Circle (KGC), which was a secret society formed in 1854 by George W. L. Bickley, a Cincinnati physician. The KGC was dedicated to supporting pro-slavery policies and promoting the American conquest of nations to the south of the USA. The purpose of this national organization was to establish a new slave empire to the south by conquering Mexico, Central America, and the Caribbean. The "golden circle" would commence in Texas and would be anchored in Key West, Florida. The Knights of the Golden Circle were allied with the Copperhead segment of the Democratic Party. They coordinated terrorist activities in the Midwest and spread throughout the North and South. By 1860 in Texas the KGC was devoted to secession, slavery, and white supremacy. The pressure for a plebiscite leading to secession was promoted by the KGC, which exercised intimidation to promote passage of the secession document. Members of this group were organized and armed prior to the outbreak of the Civil War. Friction between the secessionist officials and the Union Loyal League was substantial, but they coexisted and tolerated one another in early 1861.

By late 1861 and into 1862 this peaceful coexistence between the Union Loyal League and the secessionists began to break down as the result of several factors. Both sides had expected that the Civil War would be short lived. Many League members believed the secession was a rebellion that would be readily suppressed, and they were content to remain silent while waiting for that outcome. The League expected that Union forces would invade Texas, while the Confederacy expected that it would defeat the Union at the first major battle. The First Battle of Manassas (Bull Run) in July 1861 demonstrated that this was not to be a "90 day war." The South was victorious on the field but found it impossible to push on into the Union capital. The battle strengthened the resolve of the North to fight to the end. Both sides recognized a protracted conflict was in the offing and the romance of war was rapidly fading.

A symptom of the deteriorating relationship between the Union loyalists and the Confederate supporters was the issuance of a proclamation by Texas Governor Edward Clark.[2] It was issued in June 8, 1861, which was the same month the Union Loyal League was formed in the Hill Country. The proclamation was issued in response to the activities of Union supporters who were characterized as not being good citizens. This had come about because some Union supporters would openly celebrate Union victories by flying the U.S. flag above their homes or by shouting their approval in public. In part the proclamation provided that Texas citizens were not to be in communication with citizens of the United States. Other provisions served to isolate Texans from any commercial or financial contacts with United States citizens. The proclamation also required any citizens of any states or territories who were at war with the CSA, who were currently visiting in Texas, to leave the state within twenty days. Further, Texas Confederates were to have no friendly discussions with these visitors. While the proclamation had little deterrent effect upon Union supporters, it did serve to accelerate the breakdown of relationships. Further, this proclamation served to accent a proclamation issued by President Jefferson Davis in August 1861. The Davis proclamation stated that each person living in a Confederate state who did not profess allegiance to the CSA was to remove himself and his personal effects before October 1861.

Additionally, the Confederate Congress on April 16, 1862, passed "The Enrollment Act," which was a military draft that required all white males between the ages of eighteen and thirty-five to register for military service for three years. Texas quickly moved to implement this new law. The Hill Country Germans were adamant in their refusal to take up arms against the country to which they were loyal, and most of them intended to avoid the draft by any means. Likewise they would similarly avoid signing an oath of loyalty to the Confederacy. The odious Confederate Loyalty Oath read as follows:

> I do solemnly swear that I will faithfully and honestly support the Constitution and laws of the Confederate States of America, and I will faithfully and honestly render true allegiance to said Confederate States in all things and in every particular; and I further swear that I will not directly or indirectly, by talking, writing, or otherwise, seditiously or rebelliously attempt to excite prejudice in the mind of any person or persons against the existence, perpetaity [sic], or prosperity of said Confederate States; nor will I in any manner, directly or indirectly, aid, assist, encourage, or advise the United States, or any officer, agent, or adherent thereof, in the present war against the Confederate States (OR Ser. 1, Vol.4, 246).

Texas authorities threatened death to any individual who did not appear when called into Southern military service. The Germans were labeled as traitors, or worse. This Confederate policy of enforcing a draft and a loyalty oath had the unintended consequence of moving many Germans from neutrality or passivity in 1861 to active Union support in 1862. The more or less peaceful coexistence of 1861 was quickly moving toward armed conflict by the spring of 1862, and numerous Germans began hiding in the hills to avoid the draft.

Col. H. E. McCulloch of the Texas State troops began noting the change in the atmosphere when he wrote to his superior on March 3, 1862. He said:

> . . . I think I have discovered a pretty considerable under-current at work through this country against our cause. It does not occur to me that it can be very strong, yet it may amount in the end to something

which will require force to be used. Men have been heard to say, when we (the Confederates) lost a battle, that "We" (the Union men) "have gained a victory." Others have sent up small balloons, while others have fired guns by way of rejoicing over these victories. Others are and have been using their utmost exertions to break down the currency of the country, and some others have arms and other supplies for sale, and ask us twice as much for them in our currency as they would in gold or silver, and then refuse to let us have them unless the cash is paid in hand, although assured that they would be paid in sixty days or less. Our friends do not act in this manner, and these men are our enemies. They cannot be reached by civil law, yet they are damaging our cause every day; and if the enemy should land in force on the coast, or invade us on the north . . . it will be necessary to take charge of these men in some way . . . . Under these circumstances I look to the time that it will be necessary to declare martial law . . . (OR Ser. 1, Vol. 9, 701).

Animosity between the two sides grew and was reflected in the newspapers. The March 29, 1862, edition of the *San Antonio Herald* wrote:

It is reported . . . that the Lincolnites . . . did not even affect to conceal their pleasure upon hearing of our disasters at Forts Henry and Donaldson. . . . Away with the Lincolnites, whether domestic or imported. It is high time that all enemies should be expelled from our state (Burrier "Notes" 27).

It is ironic that the editorial comments urged expulsion of German Unionists from the state. Within six months Germans would die while trying to leave Texas.

On March 25, 1862, the statewide League organization and its local units met secretly in San Antonio to coordinate the military arm of each unit in support of the political purposes of the organization. Ernest Cramer of Comfort represented the Hill Country Union League at this meeting. Apparently the military arm had both defensive and offensive objectives. On the defensive side, the notion was to protect League members from arrest and death at the hands of Texas government officials who viewed the League as disloyal or traitorous. It was also expected that the militia would assist all members in avoiding conscription into the CSA army. On the offensive side, there was some notion of revolutionary activity or guerrilla warfare to support an expected Union invasion of Texas. However, guerrilla warfare never materialized to any extent. At the least it was expected that these local militias would join the Union army when it invaded Texas.

In the spring of 1862 in San Antonio, placards were found written in German, which were posted in prominent locations. These read in part, "German brothers, are your eyes not opened yet? Inform everybody the revolution is broke out." The bottom of the placard read, "It is a shame that Texas has such a brand. Hang them by their feet and burn them from below" (OR Ser. 1, Vol. 9, 706).

San Antonians were alarmed because seventy-three Germans there had organized themselves into an well-armed militia (Buenger 89). The March 29, 1862, edition of the *San Antonio Herald* expressed concern about invasion of Texas by Union forces and of activity by Union loyalists. In referring to the Union sympathizers, the paper said: " . . . it will be necessary to dispose of the lurking enemies in our midst" (Burrier "Notes" 29).

Likewise, the U.S. government was becoming interested in rebellious activity in the San Antonio-Austin area. On April 8, 1862, Secretary of State Seward wrote to Secretary of War Stanton that there was " . . . the prospect of a battle near Austin, Tex., between loyal and disloyal citizens of that state" (OR Ser. 1, Vol. 9, 660). On March 21 of that same year, Secretary Seward had been told by Leonard J. Pierce, the U.S. Consul at Matamoros, Mexico, that "The Union men in Texas are becoming bolder, and a battle is expected in the neighborhood of Austin and San Antonio" (OR Ser. 1, Vol. 9, 661). Obviously, friction between the two factions was escalating. Events were quickly taking a life of their own and were propelling both sides toward disaster.

The Texas governor had legislative authority to recruit frontier companies to protect citizens from Indian attacks. Jacob Kuechler of Fredericksburg was the Gillespie County surveyor and was able to receive authority to form such a company serving Gillespie, Kerr, and Kendall counties. Thus Comfort Militia, Precinct #2, consisting of thirty-nine men, was formed in Comfort on February 19, 1862 (Ransleben 102). Jacob Kuechler was chosen as captain, and the company consisted entirely of Union sympathizers, many of whom would be with him at the Nueces River in August. Secessionists were excluded. The hidden agenda of the organization was to assume defensive measures against the secessionists and to serve as the base for development of other aggressive organizations. However, the governor became aware of this misuse of his authority and ordered the company to be disbanded. It was demobilized, and this action led to the formation of the Union Loyal League's Hill Country Militia.

The timing for forming the Hill Country Militia in May was not accidental. In February 1862 Forts Henry and Donelson in Tennessee fell to Union troops as did Nashville; on March 7-8, 1862, Union forces had defeated Confederate forces at nearby Pea Ridge, Arkansas; on March 26-28 a Union army defeated a Confederate army at Glorieta Pass near Santa Fe, New Mexico; on April 6-7 the Union was victorious at the Battle of Shiloh (Pittsburgh Landing) near the Tennessee-Mississippi border; on May 1 New Orleans was occupied by Federal troops and on May 15 Baton Rouge fell; also on May 15 there was a Federal naval demonstration upon Galveston; and in July Union guerrillas smashed the Confederacy at Moore's Mills, Missouri.

This rapidly developing military activity, and Union victories near Texas, encouraged the hopes of the League and its militia that Union forces would soon invade the Lone Star State. While these Confederate setbacks encouraged the Union Loyal League, they alarmed the Confederate government in Texas.

CHAPTER 4.

THE JOURNEY

The Hill Country Militia, which had left the Turtle Creek assembly point on August 2, was now into the sixth day of its journey. The men had proceeded toward Del Rio at a leisurely pace because they felt safe and were unaware that they were being followed. Also their pack animals were heavily laden and they wished to spare their horses and mules undue hardship. Further slowing them was the fact that they shot game, gathered honey, and had to find water for their pack animals and horses. Water was an especially critical factor because the Hill Country was experiencing a drought. Many South Texas streams had become dry arroyos. On August 8 they were joined on the trail by four Anglo Texans (Howard Henderson, William Hester, Thomas J. Scott, and Warren B. Scott) which increased the size of the group to sixty-nine.

By the next afternoon they had come about ninety miles, and Maj. Fritz Tegener wished to stop on the west branch of the Nueces River. He and the guide, John Sansom, argued about stopping there for the night. Sansom thought it wise for them to press on. He believed strangers may have seen them and suggested they should leave immediately, ride all night, and cross over into Mexico. Tegener, on the other hand, was concerned about the horses for they were mostly unshod and some were lame due to the stony topography of the plateau. He wanted to rest the men and horses. Earlier in the day some members of the militia had spotted some people on a nearby hill, but they were unable to identify them. It was suggested that militia members had seen one of their own hunting parties on the nearby hill. Tegener dismissed the notion that someone might be following them. Sansom was less sure about their security. Tegener did agree to take the matter up with Captain Kuechler and Lieutenant Degener, but both these men believed no strangers were around and they wished to remain at the present camp until the next morning. That settled the matter. Major Tegener elected to make camp where they were.

Twenty-eight-year-old John W. Sansom had been born on February 5, 1834, in Alabama and had moved to Texas with his parents in 1839. His father became an Indian fighter on the frontier and the boy followed in his footsteps. By 1855, at age twenty-one, John had become an experienced defender on the frontier fighting Mexican bandits and Indians who were intent on destroying property, committing murder, stealing horses, and the like. On many occasions he had traveled in the area between the Nueces and Rio Grande rivers and on into Mexico, and he was well aware of the dangers of the region. In fact rather recent events demonstrated the danger inherent in this region. The previous summer, in late May 1861, two men had been ambushed near this campsite by about twenty Indians and were killed. Some men detached from Company F, 2nd Regiment, 1st Texas Mounted Rifles, happened upon the murder scene on June 12, 1861, and Pvt. W. W. Heartsill wrote about it in his diary. He said, "I visited and closely examined a large pecan tree under which their mutilated bodies were found. One of the men had been scalped once, the other three times and his heart had been cut out and laid on his body" (Heartsill 104). Perhaps because of his background and experience in this region, Sansom tended to be much more cautious than Major Tegener.

Tegener decided they would set up camp in a clear space near the stream. The clearing provided easy access

John W. Sansom was the guide for the Unionists in their journey toward Mexico. Later he was a captain in the Union army and a captain with the Texas Rangers.

—Private collection of Paul Burrier

to good water and also the opportunity for the light southerly evening breeze to cool the men and horses.[3] The selected campsite was described by a survivor, August Hoffman, who said, "We had a good time, that Saturday night. Camp had been pitched nearly 350 yards from the Nueces, on a fairly clear space of about an acre.

Strategically, the camp-site was a joke—being joined to the main cedarbrakes of the river bottom by a timbered strip" (Hoffman, newspaper art., n.p.). After a night of feasting on game and making patriotic speeches, the Germans retired after posting guards.

Confederates garrisoned Camp Wood after it was abandoned by Federal troops. It was the CSA outpost nearest the Nueces battlefield and was about twenty miles to the east. The Unionist force was nearby on August 7-8, 1862.

—Author's private collection

The Unionist camp was located about 150 yards to the right in this photo. —Private collection of Paul Burrier

CHAPTER 5

THE REACTION

T he Anglo Texans viewed the establishment of an armed militia as a hostile act in the Hill Country. At that time Col. Henry Eustace McCulloch, First Regiment, Texas Mounted Rifles, was stationed in San Antonio. The First Regiment of the Texas Mounted Rifles had been ordered raised by the Secession Convention in February 1861. In May 1861 the unit was transferred to the Confederate Provisional Army.

McCulloch was born in Rutherford County, Tennessee, on December 6, 1816. He and his brother, Ben, came to Texas in 1835. Ben was killed in the Civil War at the Battle of Pea Ridge. Henry was an early Texas Ranger and when the Civil War began he was appointed a Confederate colonel. He was promoted to brigadier general in 1862 (Burrier "Notes" 26). On March 25, 1862, Colonel McCulloch wrote to Col. Samuel B. Davis, as follows:

> SIR: I find that many of the most notorious among the leaders of the opposition, or Union men, are leaving the country, principally in the direction of Mexico. Some of them, I have no doubt, are going simply to avoid the draft, and under its operations a participation in the present struggle with the North, while others are going to co-operate with a considerable number that have already entered Mexico, and are now at Monterey and other points, doing all

they can to prejudice our cause with the authorities of that country, and prepare the minds of the common people to take part against us in case there ever is a time when they dare call on them to do so, and to act in concert with men of like feelings about Austin, this place, Fredericksburg, and other points where they are still living among us.

I have said, and I repeat, that there is, in my opinion, a considerable element of this character in this section that will have, ultimately (if the war becomes any more disastrous to us), *to be crushed out, even if it has to be done without due course of law,* [emphasis added] or this country—the section in which I am stationed to protect and in which my family reside—will suffer.

In view of these things I have taken steps to prevent as far as possible the passage of these men out of the country into Mexico, by instructing the military under my command not to let any man go unless he is known to be our friend, and not then unless he can produce satisfactory evidence that he is not going to avoid the draft with which the State is threatened and which will come upon it.

I am fully aware of the responsibility of the step I have taken, and how much it perils my reputation as an officer, and how much it exposes my person and my domestic interests—my home, my wife and little ones—to the malignant acts of these cowardly traitors, but I believe it my duty to my country, and in her case I am willing to peril my all.

The force that I will have congregated here in a few days more will be sufficient to enable the State authorities to enforce the draft or do anything else that a military force may be required to do, and while I assure you that I shall take no step rashly or without reflection, I shall use it for the benefit of my country upon traitors at home if needs be (OR Ser. 1, Vol. 9, 704-5).

Gen. Paul O. Hebert, in command of the Department of Texas, was to proclaim martial law within two months. Paul Octave Hebert was born on December 12, 1818, in Iberville Parish, Louisiana. He graduated first in his class of forty-two students in 1840 from the U.S. Military Academy and taught at West Point after graduation. He served in the Mexican War and from 1853 to 1856 was the governor of Louisiana. He was appointed brigadier general of state troops in 1861 and gained the same rank in the CSA Army on May 26, 1862 (Boatner 391; Wakelyn 224-5).

Hebert, in his General Orders No. 45 issued May 30, 1862, imposed martial law on the Lone Star State. The General Orders state,

> Every white male person above the age of sixteen years, being temporarily or otherwise within the aforesaid limits, shall, upon a summons issued by the provost-marshal, promptly present himself before said provost-marshal to have his name, residence, and occupation registered, and to furnish such information as may be required of him. And such as claim to be aliens shall be sworn to the effect that they will abide by and maintain the laws of this State and the Confederate States so long as they are permitted to reside therein, and that they will not convey to our enemies any information whatever or do any act injurious to the Confederate States or beneficial to the United States.
>
> Provosts-marshal shall order out and remove from their respective districts all disloyal persons and all persons whose presence is injurious to the interests of the country.
>
> All orders issued by the provosts-marshal in the execution of their duties shall be promptly obeyed. Any disobedience of summons emanating from them shall be dealt with summarily (OR Ser. 1, Vol. 9, 716).

After martial law was imposed, the people in the Hill Country were forced to take the oath of loyalty to the Confederacy or risk losing their property. Many Germans succumbed to this pressure and signed the oath. Under this intimidation some also revealed the names of the officers of the militia, which doomed these men to probable death, should they be caught. Therefore they fled to the mountains to avoid the conscription law and death. Of these times, Ernest Cramer writes, "We formed a hunting party, hunted in the mountains, and were hunted and chased by soldiers. But we knew the country and every secret path and hiding nook too well to allow ourselves to be caught" (Cramer, n.p.). The number of men in the mountains continued to grow as the pressure grew more intense. It was well known among local citizens that as many as 100 Union sympathizers may have been in hiding.

In May 1861 at the national Confederate capitol, there was discussion at the highest levels about forming partisan ranger groups in the Confederate states to maintain order as a state militia of sorts. It was also considered that they might assist active CSA Army units in guerrilla warfare. On April 21, 1862, the Confederate Congress passed the Partisan Ranger Act and under this act Duff's Texas Partisan Rangers, which was under the command of Capt. James M. Duff, became part of the CSA Army.

Duff was well known to the Confederate leadership in Texas due to his having previously distinguished himself. On April 23, 1861, he was an obscure officer in charge of a company of Texas citizen volunteers who caused a Union infantry company to surrender to him. Duff had encountered Capt. A. T. Lee's company of the Eighth U. S. Infantry, which was under the command of Lt. E. W. H. Read. The Company of Citizen Volunteers under Duff's command demanded the Union Company unconditionally surrender as prisoners of war. Lieutenant Read, after consultation with his commanding officer, did in fact surrender his troops to Captain Duff (OR Ser. 1, Vol. 1, 578). The disarming of a company of United States troops was a feather in his cap, and his superiors commended him. He was on his way toward developing a positive reputation among Confederate authorities. By the beginning of May he had been promoted to the rank of lieutenant colonel in state service and he was in command of a battalion. He came to be viewed by the Confederates as a skilled and efficient soldier.

James M. Duff was born in Perthshire, Scotland, in

1828 and arrived in the United States in 1848. On January 6, 1849, he enlisted in the Fifth Regiment, U.S. Infantry, and he was described as being "5 feet 10 inches tall with gray eyes and light brown hair" (Selcer and Burrier 57). He was sent to the frontier to deal with the Cherokees and deserted. He was later arrested and court martialed for being absent from his unit and was appropriately sentenced. However, the sentence was set aside, apparently because of extenuating circumstances, and he was pardoned. He went on to serve his unit well through his full five-year term of enlistment, and he was honorably discharged as a sergeant on January 6, 1854. After his discharge he worked closely with the army providing supplies. At the time of secession he immediately commenced his service on behalf of the Texas and Confederate military operation and quickly moved through the ranks. At the end of the war he had attained the rank of colonel.

On May 30, 1862, Brig. Gen. Paul O. Hebert, commanding the Department of Texas, ordered Captain Duff and his Rangers to go to Fredericksburg to implement his martial law proclamation. Captain Duff arrived there on the day the order was issued. He proclaimed martial law and gave the citizens six days to report to take the oath of allegiance to the Confederacy. He proceeded to identify and arrest approximately nine Union (disloyal) citizens and mentioned the creation of a disloyal military organization. In particular he singled out Jacob Kuechler and said, "Captain Keuchler I did not succeed in arresting. He was the only one . . . who had not taken the oath of allegiance. In connection with this subject I may be allowed to suggest that steps should be taken to arrest Captain Keuchler. He is a man of great influence; a German enthusiast in politics and a dangerous man in the community" (OR Ser. 2, Vol. 4, 785-87). On June 20, 1862, Duff returned to San Antonio.

The Union Loyal League was actively considering its response to these developments not realizing it had an informant in its midst by the name of Basil Stewart. He reported some of this information to Texas state officials and the League then became aware of this spy. The League decided to execute this traitor, drawing straws to select the person who would do the deed. Ernst Beseler drew the straw and shot Stewart to death on July 5, 1862. Beseler was to become the second man to die at the Nueces River on August 10, 1862.

The execution of Stewart served to further escalate tensions, and the Texas authorities became concerned about the security of Federal prisoners at Camp Verde, a few miles west of Comfort. They decided to move them to Fort Mason, about sixty miles to the north. League members discussed taking Fort Mason, arming the Federal prisoners, and going to Mexico or joining Union troops in New Mexico. Before any action could be taken, the prisoners were moved again in late July to more secure facilities in San Antonio.

In July 1862 Gen. Hamilton P. Bee was the commander of the sub-military district of the Rio Grande in San Antonio. Hamilton Prioleau Bee was born on July 22, 1822, in Charleston, South Carolina, and he and his father moved to Galveston, Texas, in 1835. In 1846 he was the secretary of the first Texas Senate, and in the 1850s he was the speaker of the third Texas House and a clerk to Governor Francis Lubbock. Bee enlisted as a private in the Mexican War and was promoted to first lieutenant in 1847. In 1861 he enlisted in the Texas militia and commanded Texas coastal troops. On March 6, 1862, he was promoted to brigadier general and was posted at Brownsville, Texas, "where he ran cotton through the Union blockade and bought munitions from Europe" (Wakelyn 95-96).

General Bee became alarmed at reports that Germans in the Hill Country were ". . . organizing and arming to resist the execution of the law known as the Conscript Act." He reported an armed force, perhaps as large as 500 armed traitors, were ". . . moving their goods and families, with large supplies of provisions, into the mountain districts. . . ." He added that they had ". . . murdered one or two well-known secession or loyal citizens." Because of these developments he appointed Captain Duff as provost-marshal and instructed him ". . . to issue a proclamation declaring martial law, and requiring all good and loyal citizens to return quietly to their homes, and take the oath of allegiance to the Confederate and State governments, or be treated summarily as traitors in arms. . . ." He also instructed Captain Duff ". . . to send out scouting parties into the mountain districts . . . to find and break up any such encampments and depots as had been reported to exist there, and to send the families and provisions back to the settlements." General Bee added that as Captain Duff was carrying out his orders ". . . it became certain that there were still many in arms who were determined to resist the Government at all hazards. Lieutenant McRae's detachment was sent on a scout after these. . . ." The general stated that Lieutenant McRae's report was attached and it detailed ". . . an engagement between a detachment of C.S. troops under his command and a body of unknown men in arms against the Government." Further it said that "Lieutenant McRae and his command behaved with admirable coolness and bravery, and did their work most effectually" (OR Ser. 1, Vol. 53, 454-55).

When Captain Duff arrived in Fredericksburg early in July, he combed the nearby hills looking for the militia leaders. In particular he kept the homes of Jacob Kuechler and Fritz Tegener under surveillance but was unable to capture them because they were in hiding in the mountains. Ernest Cramer was still hiding in the mountains too but he stated, "Early in July I had to go home. We were expecting a child. I arrived on the morning of the 10th, and on the following day we were blessed with the birth of a small daughter" (Cramer, n.p.). Captain Duff missed capturing one of the militia leaders.

It is alleged by German sources that during this period Captain Duff and his successor, in the process of carrying out these orders, brutalized many citizens of the Hill Country by arrest, burning crops and homes, and hanging and shooting dissidents. Duff came to be viewed by German Unionists as a butcher who ran a virtual reign of terror when he enforced martial law in the Hill Country

in the spring and summer of 1862. People living in that
community labeled him as "the Butcher of Fredericksburg" (Selcer and Burrier 57) and referred to his unit as
the "haengerbund" (hanging gang). On the other hand
Confederate officials thought well of him. For example, in
the fall of 1863 Gen. H. P. Bee said of his subordinate,
". . . I need not say that Colonel Duff will be indispensable
to me; there are very few such officers in Texas" (OR Ser.
1, Vol. 26, pt. 1, 396). Furthermore, at the end of the war
he was a colonel in command of the 33rd Texas Cavalry.

A more impartial view of Duff may be gained through
reviewing the journal of Lt. Col. Arthur Lyon Fremantle.
Colonel Fremantle visited Civil War America as a tourist
from English military circles. Wishing to honor the blockade that the Union had imposed, he entered the United
States through Mexico at the village of Bagdad, which was
at the mouth of the Rio Grande near Brownsville, Texas.
On April 2, 1863, the first men he encountered in Texas
were six Confederate officers who were members of Duff's
cavalry. The senior officer said that he had crossed the
river three weeks ago and had captured some renegades.
One of them was a man who was named "Mongomery" (or
"Montgomery") who had been left on the road to Brownsville (this was said with a smile on the officer's face).
Fremantle proceeded about nine miles when he met
Confederate Gen. Hamilton Bee, with whom he had a cor-
dial conversation. The colonel mentioned to the general
that he understood a man named Mongomery had been
killed. General Bee said the Mongomery affair was not
sanctioned by him, and he was sorry for it. Half an hour
later Freemantle came to the spot on the road where
Mongomery had been left and indeed he had been killed.
This had occurred on March 15, 1863. Colonel Fremantle
described the scene, "He had been slightly buried, but his
head and arms were above the ground, his arms tied
together, the rope still around his neck, but part of it still
dangling from quite a small mesquite tree. . . . I obtained
this my first experience of lynch law within three hours of
landing in America" (151).

About three miles from this spot he came upon Col. James Duff's encampment. Fremantle described Duff as a "... fine-looking, handsome Scotchman ..." (151). Fremantle learned that Mongomery had earned the ire of the Confederates because he would toss all sorts of insulting epithets at them from the Mexican side of the river. Furthermore, Mongomery's group had crossed over the river and had killed some unarmed cotton teamsters. Fremantle added, "Colonel Duff confessed that the Mongomery affair was wrong, but he added that his boys *'meant well'*" [emphasis in original] (152).

It probably is fair to say that Duff was a human being who may have displayed elements of these disparate characteristics from time to time, but people who wished to make a statement or a point emphasized the extremes in his behavior. Furthermore, one must remember that "lynch law" had been common on the Texas frontier for years before the Civil War. In any event, Duff was to become a pivotal character in what was to take place on the Nueces River.

At the same time it was reported that Union sympathizers were intimidating Confederate supporters by refusing their currency in commercial transactions, insulting them, and verbally and physically abusing them. Also, a guerrilla group known as the "Luckenbach Bushwhackers" had become engaged in more severe reprisals. Clearly the level of violence was increasing.

The members of the Union Loyal League felt it would be dishonorable to renounce their previous loyalty oath to the Union in favor of the Confederate oath. Likewise, they would not accept conscription into the CSA Army. This subjected them to possible death, their families to possible atrocities, and their property to confiscation or destruction. The situation had become untenable for them. They discussed fleeing to Mexico but they did not have the means to take their families with them. They also discussed participating in guerrilla warfare but were concerned about reprisals against their families. By July 25, 1862, Fritz Tegener, the battalion commander, had discussed their options with Eduard Degener, advisor and head of the Union Loyal League, and the decision was made that those who wished to flee to Mexico should do so.

R. H. Williams was a private in the Con-federate forces (Duff's Com-pany) that attacked the Unionist camp on the morning of August 10, 1862. This photo was taken in 1863.

—Private collection of Paul Burrier

CHAPTER 6.

THE FOLLOWERS

n August 3, 1862, Lt. Colin D. McRae left his Pedernales River camp with a detachment of ninety-four men, as ordered by Captain Duff, to scout and break up any armed encampments or depots he might find. He proceeded up the south fork of the Guadalupe River, and on the morning of August 6 he found the trail of the Germans, which he followed in a southwesterly direction for four days. It is assumed that Lieutenant McRae was told that the Germans were planning to go to Mexico and was informed as to their intended route. One source of information may have been Basil Stewart, the League member who was executed by Ernst Beseler the previous month. Another source may have been Charles Burgmann (Bergmann) from whom the Germans had stolen supplies early in their journey. Burgmann got his revenge by informing Captain Duff of the route and composition of the German party (Selcer and Burrier 63). Adolf Paul Weber wrote, "A few days after they [the militia members] had started their march, they met a German by the name of Bergmann who had fallen upon a store of provisions in an open field. Perhaps as a joke or out of hunger, they took the food away from him, for which, Bergmann, out of anger, put the pursuers on the trail of his countrymen" (13).

It was not difficult for Lieutenant McRae to pick up a trail of sixty-five men with about eighty-three horses

and mules traveling together as a military unit. The
McRae Confederate group consisted of detachments from
Donnelson's Company of the 2nd Texas Mounted Rifles,
Duff's Company of Texas Partisan Rangers, Davis' Company of Texas State troops, and Taylor's 8th Texas Cavalry Battalion. Burgmann may have continued with them
as a guide. They rode hard to catch up with the Germans.

On the afternoon of August 7 they found the smol-
dering coals of a campfire left by the group they were pursuing. McRae continued to pursue the Hill Country Militia
for two more days. At around 3:00 P.M. on August 9 an
advance guard of Lieutenant McRae's military body reported the German camp in sight on the west branch of
the Nueces River. McRae led his group to within two and
one-half miles of the militia's camp, where he set up a
camp for his men in a small canyon. He and Lieutenants
Homsley, Lilly, Harbour, and Bigham then carefully
reconnoitered Tegener's camp. They returned to their
camp in the canyon and developed a plan to attack the
next morning at daybreak.

Lieutenant McRae made no more moves until after
the moon had set at around 11:00 P.M. At about 1:00 A.M.
on August 10 he moved his command to within 300
yards of the camp and divided his force in two. One wing
under the command of Lt. James Homsley was positioned opposite the Unionists' right flank about fifty
yards away in a dense cedar-brake. The other wing under
the command of Lieutenant McRae was positioned in a
cedar-brake about forty yards away from the Unionists'
left flank. These movements were accomplished by about
3:00 A.M. However, this activity was detected by the
guard, Leopold Bauer, who fired upon the intruders and
in turn probably was killed by Lt. William T. Harbour. A
second guard, Ernst Beseler, became engaged in the firing and likewise was killed. The gunfire alerted the camp.
The German camp fired sporadically into the dark, but
Lieutenant McRae ordered his men to hold their fire. He
did so because it was too dark to organize an effec-
tive attack. Under these circumstances, it was accepted

military practice at the time to launch such an attack at sunrise.

Meanwhile, in the German camp, there was discussion, disagreement, and preparation. The discussion and disagreement was around whether to stay and fight or withdraw to a better defensive position. One group led by Fritz Tegener was determined to fight at the campsite because they considered escape impossible and to flee would mean losing their horses and rations. Lieutenant Degener exclaimed, "I would rather fight here until every man of us is killed than to go anywhere else" (Sansom "Battle" 9). Apparently Capt. Jacob Kuechler had reservations about the defensibility of the selected position, for he later wrote, "Our position was not good and could not be improved" (Kuechler, n.p).

Another side led by John Sansom thought it wise to withdraw to a better defensive position. Sansom said, ". . . they out-number us greatly, and they have a much better position than we. For these reasons we ought to withdraw" (Sansom "Battle" 9).

The two sides agreed to disagree. The Tegener group decided to stay at the original site and fight until death if necessary. They began improving their position at the campsite by making a wall with equipment such as saddles and flour sacks.

At this point, the Sansom side began withdrawing into the hills, or obtaining better positions. This side consisted of twenty-three Germans plus one group consisting of John Sansom and the four Anglo Texans who had joined the larger unit on the trail on August 8. The five-man Sansom group had in mind outflanking the attackers, and they went to the rear and then the side.

Sixty-nine men were in the camp when the group went to sleep on August 9. Around 3:00 A.M. two guards were killed. Sometime after the 3:00 A.M. gunfire and before the Confederate sunrise attack on August 10, twenty-eight men (the five Anglos and twenty-three Germans) withdrew from the campsite to defensive positions at the rear and flanks, or left the battle site. This left thirty-nine Germans in their positions to defend against the Confederate attack. Lieutenant McRae's group of dismounted cavalry consisted of ninety-four men.

Near sunrise, at around 6:00 A.M. on that Sunday morning, Lieutenant McRae's group attacked the defenders after advancing under cover to within thirty yards of the German line. Lieutenant McRae had deployed his two wings to the north/northeast and to the south/southwest of the Germans' defensive position. Both wings then charged and the detachment fired their breech-loading rifles into the massed Germans. The Germans defended themselves as best they could, and their resistance was stiff. There were several charges and counterattacks and the battle went on for some time. Early in the action Maj. Fritz Tegener, the battalion commander, suffered three gunshot wounds but he managed to escape capture or death. Because Tegener's severe wounds disabled him, twenty-three-year-old Amil Schreiner assumed command. Schreiner was a farmer and tanner who had been born in France. At one point during the battle he cried out, "Let us sell our lives as dearly as we can" (Ransleben 88) and he led a counterattack. They did sell their lives dearly for their newly adopted country to which they had immigrated between 1845 and 1858.

CHAPTER 7.

ORIGINS

ne of the "Germans" taking a stand in their defensive positions was Pablo Diaz. He was an anomaly in the sense that he was the only man there who did not have a German surname. Diaz was born in Mexico about 1840, but German families raised him. He was reported to be a servant in the household of William Marschall in Gillespie County when he was eighteen years of age. On the journey across the Edwards Plateau and the Hill Country, he was a messmate of John Sansom. Although a Mexican, he was considered by all to be as "German" and "Unionist" as any of the others. The other thirty-eight men were born in Germany and most of them had immigrated to the United States of America between 1848 and 1858. They all had complex reasons for immigrating to Texas, but common threads were freedom and opportunity for bettering their lives.

Another of these defenders was August Hoffman who was typical of the rest. He was born in the village of Lichtenau, Silesia, Germany, on December 9, 1842. His father was a textile worker and he weaved articles for sale. August's apprentice job was to fill the shuttles and he made four napkins a week. The boy's mother died when he was nine. At this time a number of his father's friends had left for America, and the father began to realize that the future for him in Germany was none too bright. When

August was twelve years old his father sold everything, and in August 1854 he and his son took a sailing ship from Germany to New Orleans, Louisiana. There were 365 passengers on board, and the boy helped the cook by carrying the lanterns into the hold to get provisions. After a nine-week trip they arrived on American soil and between them they had fifteen cents. They got work in New Orleans through a German immigration house. The father worked as a carpenter and August ". . . found a job setting up ten-pins at a bowling alley." His work was to sweep out and clean the alley. He worked from 9:30 A.M. until 4:00 A.M. and got two meals. August reported, "I received quite a few tips because I was pretty fast in placing the pins" (Hoffman "Letter," n.p.).

He and his father worked in New Orleans for two months to save enough money to take another sailing ship to Indianola, Texas, on the Gulf Coast. When getting off the boat August stated, ". . . a man asked us where we were going, and when father told him Fredericksburg, he said 'well, I wish you very good luck but I am afraid you will be scalped by the Indians'" ("Letter" n.p.). Three weeks later father and son arrived in Fredericksburg and they eventually lived in separate German homes. August attended school and worked as a teamster hauling freight with adult men. He was hauling freight on his own when the Civil War broke out.

The Hoffman story is similar to those of the other German men in the defensive group. They had all endured hardship in Germany and were looking forward to a new life in America. They were all leaving a nation that had experienced extreme turmoil, but they were proud of their Germanic heritage.

Modern Germany consists of four regions. One is the Great Plain, which extends across Europe from the Netherlands to the Ural Mountains in Russia. The Mid-German Uplands in the south constitute a second region. This region's topography consists of hills and valleys, and a prominent feature is the Rhine River. Another region farther south is the Bavarian Plateau and Bavarian Alps.

A mountainous region, one of its prominent features is the beautiful Danube River. A fourth region is the North German Plain that is flat in the east and hilly in the west. There are areas of marshes along the coast of the North Sea with sandy heath and moorlands inland. In the northwest portion of the plain, the Elbe and Ems rivers empty into the coastal marshes of the North Sea.

The plains are humid and cool and the conditions are excellent for farming, particularly dairy farming and livestock raising. Many Germans emigrated to Texas from the port of Bremen, which is located in the Lower Saxony region. Another nearby port from which they emigrated was Antwerp in Belgium.

The German people constitute the largest ethnic group in Europe west of Russia. Although nomads roamed through Europe earlier, the first sedentary settlements occurred around 3000 BC. Originally these peasants migrated from southeast Europe. Teutonic warriors, who may have come from Northern Europe, closely followed them. Racial composition became mixed due to the movements of diverse groups through Germany.

At the beginning of our era, Germanic tribes migrated to the west and south and began populating the Mediterranean region, where they clashed with the Roman Empire. In turn, the expanding Roman Empire moved into Germany and tried to contain it by building a fortification line between the Rhine and Danube rivers. The Roman Empire subsequently became weaker, and these Germanic tribes spread into France and the Balkans by AD 400. This migration and competition continued and there followed a unification of all Germanic holdings in Europe under the leadership of Charlemagne, whom the Pope had crowned as emperor of the Holy Roman Empire in AD 800. During this time of stabilization, the German settlers became less migratory and more sedentary, and much progress and development was accomplished. But after the death of Charlemagne in AD 814, unification dissolved, and tribal nobility ruled the territory. Through the AD 843 Treaty of Verdun and the rise of feudalism, the eastern part of the

Holy Roman Empire became Germany and it was cut into five duchies: Saxony, Franconia, Bavaria, Swabia, and Lorraine. Nevertheless expansion and consolidation of gains continued and the foundations of modern Germany were laid.

Feudalism, war, and religious conflict all served to contribute to the decline of the Roman Empire, and in turn the five German duchies were split into hundreds of smaller states, principalities, and dukedoms. This created a number of problems. Germany and most of Europe had become a feudalistic society. Feudalism was the social system of rights and obligations based on land ownership. The nobles, such as counts or dukes, were owners of the lands on which the people lived. The nobleman granted protection to the people living on his land and they, in turn, were serfs who were in a position of servitude to the nobleman. The feudalistic system often took advantage of the peasant who was in a position of involuntary servitude, and he began desiring freedom from the abuses of the system. However, in the absence of a strong central government these small kingdoms flourished. This brought on political chaos, which presaged the great revolution that was to occur early in the sixteenth century, for the peasant longed for a strong central government that might bring peace and prosperity.

In fact, not only Germany but also much of Europe was suffering through similar discontent. France, Germany's neighbor to the east, had been involved in the Hundred Years War with England from AD 1337 to AD 1453. The underlying cause of this war was the feudal system and economic distress. The suffering that France endured was to strengthen her spirit of nationalism that later would produce revolutionary activity. England suffered not only the Hundred Years War, but also the Wars of the Roses from AD 1455 to AD 1458. This was a series of civil wars that arose from a power struggle for the English throne.

One of the greatest of all revolutions began in 1517, when Martin Luther initiated the Reformation by rejecting the authority of the Pope. At the beginning of the sixteenth century western Europe had a single religion—Roman Catholicism. The Reformation was a stormy, often brutal conflict that split the Christians of Europe who were forced to choose between the Protestant and Catholic faiths. The Reformation flourished because of the uneasy political situation in Europe. Widely different groups from princes to peasants supported the revolt because they were not content with their present lives, and this provided them a motive for breaking from established ties.

The Reformation has been called one of the crucial turning points in history because it destroyed religious unity. Once this unity disintegrated, people began looking at their own regional interests. From this there arose new political, social, and economic problems, as well as new beliefs and opportunities. This unsettled condition led to other revolutions and wars, and these events eventually encouraged German immigration to the United States.

One of the earliest of the wars of the Reformation period was the Peasant War in Germany in 1525. It was unlike earlier wars of the period because it was not just a religious war. It also had elements of a socio-economic conflict. This war was a series of local revolts against oppression of workers and lack of religious freedom. The peasants had been bound by serfdom within a feudal society and were now exploited as workers. They had an inordinate tax burden, found themselves in poor working conditions, and were brutalized (broken on the wheel, drawn and quartered, fingers chopped off, right of first night with wife or daughter, and other such atrocities). Additionally, the nobleman imposed his religion upon them. All this led the peasants to make twelve formal demands of nobility, two of which were: "The First Article. –First, it is our humble petition and desire, and also our will and resolution, that in the future we should have the power and authority so that each community should choose and appoint a pastor . . ." and "The Third Article. –It has been the custom hitherto for men to hold us as their own property . . . it is consistent with Scripture that we should be free and wish to do so" (Engels 12 Art., n.p.).

The twin desires of religious freedom and freedom from slavery were cornerstones of the peasant revolt. However, German nobles put down this revolt, which paralleled the German revolution of 1848.

The Holy Roman Empire continued to decline partially as a result of the religious revolt against the Roman Catholic Church. Finally in 1555, at the Peace of Augsburg, each German prince was given the authority to choose either Catholicism or Lutheranism for his kingdom, but this did not still the religious conflict. Instead there developed another major event impacting Germany—the Thirty Years War from 1618 to 1648. This was a series of conflicts that initially were religious disputes between Protestants and Roman Catholics. They soon developed into a struggle for political power. This war involved much of Europe and was especially brutal. Finally peace was achieved on October 24, 1648, and a confederation of princes was established. However, Germany had suffered terribly. Her population was reduced by more than half, education and agriculture were halted, religious unity was not achieved, and there were few people left to rebuild and replant. A period of stabilization followed as Prussia rose in power and created a military state. Frederick II made Prussia a leading power in Europe. However, the discontent of the peasants remained.

This dissatisfaction smoldered while a number of revolutionary activities were occurring in various nations in Europe. The French Revolution erupted with the storming of the Bastille in Paris on July 14, 1789. The French revolted primarily to achieve social and economic equality. These and other inequalities were common in Germany and throughout much of Europe, and consequently the French Revolution was a forerunner for other revolutionary activity. For example, the French revolutionary ideas of individual rights and freedom of expression led to insurgency against the monarchy in Italy in 1800.

Probably the most important document of the French Revolution was the Declaration of the Rights of Man, which contained some of the features of our own Declaration of Independence and Bill of Rights. The French sacrificed their political liberty when they accepted the rule of Napoleon I. The Napoleonic era from 1798 to 1814 helped to keep all of Europe in turmoil. Napoleon carried his wars into Germany but Prussia helped defeat him at Leipzig in 1813. At the Congress of Vienna in 1815, several hundred German states were reduced to thirty-nine, each ruled by an autocrat and grouped into a loose German Confederation. Austria and Prussia both attempted to control the Confederation. This introduced a period of political agitation that was led by liberal German university students. Social and economic discontent had produced political unrest, and the goal of the liberals was unification of Germany under a democratic government. By the 1830s this liberal movement was met with repression by the nobility, but it was the precursor of the 1848 revolt. Early versions of capitalism were destroying feudalism.

During the 1840s overpopulation and insufficient farmland to feed the people plagued Germany. The small farmer was being squeezed out by the industrial revolution. There was widespread poverty, jobs were scarce, and laborers were poorly paid. Under the oppressive rule by the church, there was significant inequality in tax assessment. In other words, many of the same conditions that spawned the Peasant Revolt of 1525 extended into this period. Additionally, drought and a potato blight in Europe led to diminished food production and widespread starvation in Germany. Perhaps one million people died in the world as a result of the 1846 Irish potato famine.

During this period, Germany was a collection of independent kingdoms, and nobility ruled with an iron fist. In this autocracy the king dictated how his people were to worship, he impressed them into his armies, he imposed unjust taxation, and he gave them no voice in determining their own destinies. The people looked around them and found other nations, most notably France, making progress toward a democratic form of government. The situation was pregnant for a revolt, which commenced in 1848. This revolutionary movement ultimately failed and

Germany was not unified under a democratic government at this time. However, the forces that led to the movement stimulated increased immigration to the United States of America and particularly to Texas. It also produced a core of Germans who were to become loyal to the concept of a strong central government and to a democracy as represented by the United States of America and its Constitution, which was held by them to be a revered document. This same core would find a confederation of Southern states to be anathema because of their own negative experiences with a confederation of German states.

CHAPTER 8.

THE IMMIGRANTS

erman immigration to the United States began long before we became a nation. One hundred years before the Declaration of Independence, William Penn traveled to Europe and learned that thousands of people of the Quaker faith were eager to immigrate to the United States to escape religious persecution. Mr. Penn was successful in securing a land grant to the "Province of Pennsylvania," and he laid out the town of Philadelphia. Nearby Germantown came to be populated with Germans of mostly the Mennonite sect. (Interestingly, the Quakers in Germantown in 1688 denounced slavery.) Through the eighteenth century, German immigration continued to the Philadelphia area and that city became the port of entry for people of different nationalities. In time some of the German groups began moving westward, as did others. This movement initially was into the Western Reserve and later further west into Indiana, Illinois, Kentucky, and Tennessee. The first significant groups of Germans did not appear in Texas until early in the nineteenth century.

Various settlers began coming to Texas in the early 1820s because the Mexican government encouraged immigration with generous land grants. *Empresario* colonies were formed in Texas while it was under Mexican rule. This term was used to describe granting of land for colonization. Contracts were made to designate colonies

🪶 55

and bring settlers to the Texas frontier. There were several important early colonizations. Baron de Bastrop obtained grants, one of which was located at Comal Springs in the Hill Country of Texas between the Brazos and Colorado rivers where New Braunfels was founded. Permission was granted to bring 300 families there in 1821. Another grant to bring 300 families to the vicinity of present-day Austin was made to Stephen F. Austin in 1823. Other settlers during this period came to Galveston, Nacogdoches, San Antonio, and Houston.

Liberal land grants stimulated settlement in these areas. For example, for those arriving before March 2, 1836, at a Bastrop grant, 4,605 acres of land was granted to the head of a family while single men received 1,476 acres. Generally, title to the land was received after certain conditions were met (such as farming, raising cattle, erecting a building) within a specified time frame. Each family arriving at the Austin site received 177 acres of rich land suitable for cultivation and 13,000 acres of prairie pasture. The size of these grants decreased in later years.

These early colonies prospered. By 1834 the Austin colony consisted of 22,000 people, one-tenth of whom were Negro slaves. The Southern planters in the area found they could not prosper without the use of slaves. However, the Mexican Congress declared in 1831 that slavery was abolished and that all settlers were to be Roman Catholics. Austin, Bastrop, and others were able to disregard these decrees with impunity until 1835 when Mexico proclaimed a unified constitution that eliminated these "states' rights." In December 1835 Texans announced their intent to secede from Mexico rather than give up their "right" to slavery. The twin issues of Catholicism and slavery triggered the secession of Texas from Mexico.

The Texans established a provisional government and expelled the Mexican garrison from the fortress in San Antonio—the Alamo. President Santa Anna sent Mexican troops to recapture San Antonio and on March 6, 1836, at the Alamo, the Texas defenders were all killed or wounded, and the wounded were later executed. Mexican troops were defeated the next month at the San Jacinto River, and the independent Republic of Texas was proclaimed. The new constitution of the Republic legalized slavery, and the United States recognized the Lone Star Republic on March 3, 1837.

The Republic of Texas encouraged settlers to immigrate in order to preserve its borders against Mexico's attempts to reclaim its northern boundaries. The disputed land lay between the Nueces River (to the north) and the Rio Grande (to the south). Mexico claimed its northern border to be the Nueces River, while Texas claimed its southern border to be the Rio Grande. Through 1842 and 1843 Texas and Mexico were engaged in ongoing land disputes with each side making brief incursions into the other's territory. This struggle for freedom drew many idealistic German men. These men, who were seeking freedom from oppression in Germany, believed their dreams could be fulfilled in Texas. A bit of "wanderlust" drew them as well.

One of the early settlement efforts by the Republic involved Castro's colony located southwest of San Antonio. In 1842 Sam Houston entered into a contract with Henri Castro to colonize this tract. The usual arrangement for these types of colonies was that the contractor would receive ten sections of land, and other considerations, for each 100 colonists introduced. The colonist would receive 640 acres for a head of a family (320 acres for a single man) with the requirement that fifteen acres be placed into cultivation within a certain time before the deed was transferred to him. Germans, Alsatians, and Swiss settled the Castro colony, and by 1847 there were 2,134 individuals. Not all of them remained, since some were unable to meet the cultivation requirement because of Indian attacks.

Meanwhile, pressure was growing for the independent Republic of Texas to be annexed by the United States of America and become a state. In the United States, the delicate balance of power was beginning to unravel on the matter of slavery. There were thirteen free and thirteen slave states when the Republic was recognized. However, three free territories (Iowa, Minnesota, and Wisconsin) would soon be gaining admission as free states, and more would follow in the West when the "Indian problem" was resolved.

Southerners were alarmed at this impending enlargement of free states, and persuasion was exerted to admit Texas to the Union as a slave state. Slaveholders hoped this might be the springboard for expanding slavery to the Pacific Ocean. This matter was too explosive to be dealt with in the 1830s, but it would not go away. Great Britain agreed to guarantee Texan independence if the Republic would abolish slavery. This alarmed everyone. The United States did not want England to get a wedge in the middle of the continent, and the Southern politicians were panicked at the thought of repudiation of slavery in Texas. These and other cross currents moved the Union toward the 1845 annexation of the Republic of Texas. She became the twenty-eighth state of the Union on December 29, 1845.

In 1846 the United States declared war on Mexico over a territorial dispute and other matters. Mexico was defeated in 1848 and ceded vast amounts of land to the United States. A number of German men participated in this war, many of them settled permanently and, as veterans, they received generous land grants. Prior to the Mexican War, books in German describing Texas were published and read in the eastern United States and Germany. This helped to stimulate immigration. These new citizens usually settled in areas developed by other Germans, and they were able to buy land cheaply.

The bulk of German immigration into Texas occurred after the formation of the *Adelsverein* in Germany. The *Adelsverein*, loosely translated, is "The Society of Noblemen." This organization was formed on April 20, 1842, by a group of noblemen in Bebrich on the Rhine River in Germany. The *Adelsverein* issued stock shares that could be purchased only by noblemen, and this became the means of funding the organization. The organization was publicized as a group promoting the immigration of German citizens to the Republic of Texas and its stated objectives were:

- to improve the lot of the working class who are without employment, thus controlling their increasing poverty;
- to unite the emigrants by giving them protection through this Association in order to ease their burden by mutual assistance;
- to maintain contacts between Germany and the emigrants, and to develop maritime trade by establishing business connections;
- to find a market for German crafts in these settlements, and to provide a market in Germany for the products of these colonies (Lich 18).

The Society was reorganized on March 25, 1844, due to financial problems that persisted because the Society had underestimated expenses and was underfunded. It was renamed "The Society of the Protection of German Immigrants to Texas."

In Germany citizens were living in poverty and they were starving. That country was overpopulated, jobs were scarce, and wages were low. There was insufficient food available to adequately feed the populace. Because of these factors and a rigid class system, the opportunity to improve one's lot in life was minimal. Many were chafing under this lack of opportunity and the requirement of compulsory military service. Further they wished a more democratic form of government, where they might participate in decisions affecting their destiny. They wanted to vote, choose their own religion, organize trade unions, write a constitution, and get out from under the yoke of a dictatorship. In short they wished freedom and full citizenship. In Texas they saw an opportunity to obtain land cheaply and live within a unified nation, rather than a fragmented nation, and under a liberal constitution. They also were attracted by relatively high wages in Texas.

German sovereigns saw an opportunity to respond to

this need and to make a profit at the same time. The nobility had a dream of establishing a German trade colony in Texas, perhaps a "Republic of German Texas." They hoped they might export cotton, tobacco, rice, sugar, corn, and hides from Texas in exchange for manufactured goods from Germany. They were aware that Texas had the subtropical climate and soil that was well suited for growing these crops which could not be produced in Germany due to climatic incompatibility. Cotton had become an especially important crop for importation to Europe, and the Germans hoped they would be able to profit in the cotton cartel.

The *Adelsverein* also was concerned that the hunger and poverty of the common people and their agitation for political reform was a breeding ground for revolution. They had seen nobility overthrown in other revolutions. To preserve their privileged position, it occurred to the *Adelsverein* that it might be in their interest to get the unemployed, and those who agitated for political reform, out of the country. Their unstated goal was to send boatloads of German troublemakers to Texas and fill the boats with bales of cotton for their return trip to Europe. The cotton represented potential for enormous profits.

Immediately after its organization, the *Adelsverein* got moving by putting one of the members, Prince Carl of Solms-Braunfels, into a leadership position (later he was designated as commissioner-general). One of his first moves was to go to the Training School of Darmstadt, where a number of radical liberals (agitators) were located. There he recruited forty of these liberals to immigrate to Texas. These men came to be known as "The Forty," and many of them settled in the Hill Country at Bettina, which was north of Fredericksburg on the Llano River. Here they hoped to fulfill their dreams of a communistic utopia. Later on, other dissidents were recruited from the University of Halle, which was a breeding ground for new or unconventional ideas. The University of Halle's motto was "Freedom of Everything" and it educated many freethinkers (*Freidenkers*) who were absorbing communism as promulgated by Karl Marx and Frederick Engels. Many of the freethinkers settled in Comfort. All these men were to become important players in the Nueces River affair.

While people were being recruited in Germany to come to Texas, some *Adelsverein* officials had come to Texas in 1842 to purchase land and prepare for the arrival of the immigrants. They purchased land on the Colorado River near the present town of LaGrange between Houston and Austin and named it Nassau Farm. The officials returned to Germany and recommended that the first immigrants proceed to that location. It was expected that Nassau Farm would be used as the first rest station by the immigrants on their trip to the site they would settle. It was recognized that a large amount of land would be required, and in June 1844 the Society purchased an interest in a land grant consisting of three million acres between the Llano and Colorado rivers in Central Texas. This land was purchased from Henry Francis Fisher and Burchard Miller, and consequently it became known as the Fisher-Miller grant. Prince Carl of Solms-Braunfels was sent to Texas and arrived in Galveston in July 1844. Problems began piling up for him. When Commissioner Solms-Braunfels went to inspect the Fisher-Miller grant, he found it was unlivable because it was controlled by Comanches who did not take a liking to white men and would kill them.

Prince Carl then contracted with a surveyor to find more suitable land. On March 15, 1845, Prince Solms-Braunfels bought 1,265 acres of land for $1,111 on the Comal and Guadalupe rivers nearly 200 miles west of Galveston. Not surprisingly, the settlement was named "New Braunfels," after the Prince's hometown. Since the town site was westward of initial plans, it was decided the immigrants arriving at Galveston would be transshipped down the Gulf Coast to a nearer port which Prince Carl was inspired to name "Carlshaven" (the town was renamed Indian Point and then Indianola). Carlshaven was chosen because of its easy access by ocean going vessels. Schooners of moderate draft could get to the wharves without difficulty. The town was laid out on a beach of about a mile in length and consisted of two parallel streets.

In the meantime he made arrangements for the first German immigrants to depart from Bremen, Germany. In Germany they were required to enter into a contract with the Society. Portions of this instrument are of interest. In the 1844 General Regulations of the Society, it was required that all immigrants who settled in Texas, and who were males between the ages of seventeen and fifty, were "to be formed into a militia company [to protect] life and property" (Biesele 88). Apparently the concept of an armed militia was ingrained in the German culture.

Also, the regulations provided that the immigrants, upon payment of fees, were given provisional title to Texas land consisting of 320 acres if married or 160 acres if single. The immigrant was required to live on the designated land for three consecutive years, fence and cultivate fifteen acres, build a dwelling on the property, and ". . . submit in his conduct to the rules of the Society and the laws of the land" (Lich 21). The land was then his.

The first immigrants arrived at Carlshaven in December 1844 and remained housed in tents until logistical problems could be resolved. The people had a long journey by boat and typically the trip across the Atlantic took three months or so. Often they became ill because of poor nourishment, or they would contract communicable diseases. Upon arrival they needed to rest up, be well fed, have their medical conditions treated and otherwise prepare for the trip to the selected site. They then set out on their journey and established a route that was followed by later immigrants—from Carlshaven to Victoria, Gonzales and Seguin, and then to New Braunfels. These first immigrants arrived at New Braunfels on Easter, 1845. Several hundred people arrived in New Braunfels that spring. The immigration continued, and by the end of the year 4,000 people lived there. Unfortunately perhaps 500 of them died from disease in the spring and summer of 1846.

The new city was to have a major impact on the development of German settlement in the Hill Country. It was the "jump-off place," and this new town contributed to economic growth, religion, organized public education, and preservation of the German culture. This ethnic bond was a source of strength and support for the newcomers who were facing a new way of life. Some leaders feared dilution of this ethnic bond and encouraged isolation from Anglo Texans. This closeness served a purpose in 1845-1846 but would become a contributing factor to suspicion and distrust between German Texans and Anglo Texans in the future. By 1854 Frederick Olmsted had visited the Hill Country and noted that "in social and political relations, the Germans . . . mingle little with the Americans, except for the necessary buying and selling. The manners and ideal of the Texans and of the Germans are hopelessly divergent and the two races have made little acquaintance . . ." (431). On the other hand, Germans who settled in the eastern counties of Texas tended to assimilate the Anglo culture to a greater degree, and there tended to be a blend of the German and Anglo cultures in those areas.

Many of these Anglo Texans had come to the Hill Country for some of the same reasons as the Germans. They had migrated either from the Appalachian South or from the Ozark-Ouachita area of Missouri and Arkansas. The migration of the southern mountaineer of Appalachia or Ozarkia to the Texas hills was stimulated in part by the perception that these hills were topographically similar to the places from which they had migrated. It was beautiful country, especially in the spring. Frederick Olmsted said that the countryside was " . . . a rolling sheet of the finest grass, sprinkled thick with bright, many-hued flowers, with here and there a live-oak and an occasional patch of mesquite trees . . . The Medina [river] is the very ideal of purity. The road crosses upon white limestone rocks, which give a peculiar brilliancy to its emerald waters" (275-6).

New Braunfels began to prosper through the hard work of the new settlers. Less than ten years later it was viewed with favor by a visitor who said, "The main street of the town . . . was very wide—three times as wide, in effect, as Broadway in New York. The houses, with which it was thickly lined on each side for a mile, were small, low cottages, of no pretensions to elegance, yet generally looking neat and comfortable. Many were furnished with verandahs and gardens, and the greater part were either stuccoed or painted" (Olmsted 142-43).

Prince Carl was not an especially able administrator and the Society had an initial problem of having invested a large sum of money in land that was not available because of its being controlled by hostile Indians. The Society was undercapitalized from the outset and its costs exceeded projections. The organization had counted on further funding by the nobility of Germany on the speculation that a "Republic of German Texas" might be founded. However, this dream was wrecked when Texas was annexed by the United States and became a state on December 29, 1845. Consequently additional funding was not forthcoming. Finally, Prince Carl did not like what he saw was happening among the German immigrants. They were holding town hall meetings and conducting a form of democracy by voting on issues affecting their future. Prince Carl decided to return to the comfort of his monarchy, and he left Texas for his castle in Germany.

The work of the "Society of the Protection of German Immigrants to Texas" was placed under the able leadership of John O. Meusebach, who was a graduate of the University of Halle. He was a good administrator, dealt well and fairly with the immigrants, and was liberal in his social philosophy. He enjoyed the notion of being involved in a democratic movement. John Meusebach began to bring order out of chaos and, among other things, he developed new lines of credit. Additional funding was made available so that the German immigration could continue, and continue it did. Between October 1845 and April 1846, thirty-six ships carrying over 5,000 immigrants left Bremen and arrived in Galveston and Indian Point. Those who came in this period fared well, but those arriving later met disaster.

In April 1846 war broke out between the United

States and Mexico and the U.S. Army took control of all forms of transportation in support of the war effort. Over 4,000 immigrants were left on the Gulf Coast beaches without suitable shelter and insufficient food and water. Disease—mainly cholera but also typhoid fever and malaria—took the lives of 1,400 of the immigrants. Hundreds of people left their possessions on the beaches and began a 200-mile walk to New Braunfels, and more died en route.

New Braunfels was becoming congested, and immigrants were bringing disease with them and infecting earlier residents of the town. Mr. Meusebach determined that the original Fisher-Miller land grant, about eighty miles away, could be settled, and he made a major effort to enter into peaceful relationships with the Comanches in that area. This effort culminated in a treaty on the San Saba River on May 9, 1847, with the Comanche chiefs Kotemoczy, Santanna, and Mopechnicope, and that treaty brought peace. Through his diplomatic efforts with the Indians in 1846, he had been able to survey the new town of Fredericksburg, which was founded in May 1846. Meusebach also was able to secure some scarce transportation and began settling the immigrants. Diseases that the people carried with them killed over 700 people, and in January 1847 the population of Fredericksburg was only 500 persons. But after a year or so the town began to prosper. By the end of 1846 there were 7,000 German immigrants in Texas, and most of them were in the Hill Country. More were on the way and the towns of New Braunfels and Fredericksburg served as way stations into the Texas Hill Country.

In 1854 Frederick Olmsted traveled through Texas and he was not particularly positively impressed until he lived with the Germans in the Hill Country. For example, he found a contrast in food. Earlier, in the eastern part of Texas, a typical supper had consisted of "pork, fresh and salt, cold corn-bread, and boiled sweet potatoes" (60). Of dinner in a German home he wrote, "An excellent soup is set before us, and in succession there follow two courses of meat . . . two dishes of vegetables, salad, compote of peaches, coffee with milk, wheat bread from the loaf, and beautiful and sweet butter . . . "(144). He added, "We then spent an hour in conversation with the gentlemen who were in the room. They were all educated, cultivated, well-bred, respectful, kind, and affable men. All were natives of Germany, and had been living several years in Texas" (144-45).

W. W. Heartsill was a member of the W. P. Lane Rangers which later became a company of the Confederate 2nd Regiment, 1st Texas Mounted Rifles. He passed through New Braunfels on May 6, 1861, to have his horse shod. He stated, "The inhabitants of this town were exclusively German, and I have never been treated better in my life" (Heartsill 100).

Two earlier arrivals in the Live Oak Creek area of Gillespie County were eleven-year-old Jacob Heinrich Usener and his four-year-old brother, Louis (Ludwig Wilhelm) Usener. They had arrived with their parents aboard the ship *Semiramus* at Indianola, Texas, on August 10, 1845. They too were with August Hoffman when the initial German group departed for Mexico in August 1862.

Another early arrival was Jacob Kuechler. He was one of "The Forty" who arrived in Texas in 1847 and was considered a "Revolutionary." He moved to Gillespie County (Fredericksburg) in the mid-1850s and was elected captain of that county's company in the Union Loyal League Militia. Kuechler was a leader in both the battle at the Nueces River in August 1862 and at the skirmish at the Rio Grande in October 1862.

From 1845 on, Germany was emptying itself of the unemployed as a way of dealing with poverty and ridding itself of the intelligentsia as a method of dealing with the threat of revolution. Some historians speculate that the 1848 revolution in Germany against the monarchy failed because most of the revolutionaries had been shipped to Texas. The intelligentsia were highly educated university students, many of whom were from the University of

Halle, John Meusebach's school. These were idealistic and often impractical young men who were absorbing the basic concepts of communism. Karl Marx was their hero, and his Communist Manifesto was published in 1848. These students viewed communism as a possible means of replacing the dictatorship of the German monarchy. Additionally, many of them became interested in democracy as an alternative and had studied the United States Constitution and Bill of Rights. They urged revolution and hoped the unemployed and disenchanted would join with them in causing the overthrow of the nobility as had been the case in France and Italy. Most of these freethinkers began arriving in the Texas Hill Country from 1845 on and began testing their theories.

These university students tended to stay together in small communes, where they implemented their utopian schemes of holding things in common. This communal living was one aspect of the idealistic form of communism. The communes often did not work out well because the students were impractical dreamers who "talked the talk" but shunned farming, weaving and building—necessary tasks for frontier survival. Most of the intellectuals wanted to give directions and few wanted to do the work. Where an alliance of workers and intellectuals developed, a small community would spring up. The principal small communities that arose in the Hill Country were Bettina, Comfort, Sisterdale, and Tusculum, which today is Boerne. Bettina was the first of these communities and it was established in 1847. The freethinkers came here with few practical frontier skills, and they would tend to engage in philosophical debates and quibble about work. This communistic utopia did not work out, and the town declined.

However, some other communities of a like nature did thrive because there was a melding of the impractical intelligentsia with the practical worker, craftsman, and businessman. The community of Tusculum evolved into the thriving community of Boerne. Sisterdale was a small but successful community that attracted "The Forty-

Eighters" who were refugees from the 1848 revolution in Germany. Frederick Olmsted said, "Sisterdale is a settlement of eight or ten farms . . . upon the Guadalupe, at the junction of the Sister creeks and the crossing of the Fredericksburg road. The farmers are all men of education, and have chosen their residences . . . within social distance of one another . . . [They are] a sort of political hermits, who have retired into the woods, and live with one companion, or in complete solitude" (191). An early settler of Sisterdale was Eduard Degener who lost two sons at the Nueces River affair and later became a well-known political figure in Texas. Nearby Comfort became the focal point for freethinkers.

Comfort and Sisterdale were called "Latin settlements," because the men would often sit around at night in a home library to sing German songs and hold political discussions in Latin, which was the formal language used in the university classroom. It was people from these communities and the environs who were heavily represented among those killed at the Nueces River.

The town of Comfort was settled by German immigrants in 1852 and two years later Ernst Altgelt, a twenty-one-year-old lawyer who had been born in Prussia, laid out 300 town lots and established a gristmill. It is said a small group, weary from their travels from New Braunfels, was so pleased with the picturesque spot and good water that they named it "Camp Comfort." Other lore suggests that Mr. Altgelt hoped settlers there would live their life in "comfort," which is ironic considering the tragic death of the youth of the town. In any event, this "Latin settlement" attracted a group of university students and well-educated men who had common interests in the arts, philosophy, and politics. Disillusioned with the world, they sought to isolate themselves here in order to pursue their quest for learning. Comfort became the center of radical thinking and activity that led to the flight to Mexico in August 1862.

These freethinkers had left Germany to escape political persecution and religious oppression, and they tended to be agnostics or atheists. In the early years of the community of Comfort, nearly all residents were freethinkers. Because of their influence, "From 1849 to 1892, 43 years, no church was built in our community. In very few of the homes was there a Bible or any religious literature. There were no prayers. At funerals sentimental German ballads were sung" (Observations of Vera Flach, Lich 135). Guido Ransleben had a contrasting observation when he stated that religious services were "held in homes or other suitable places" (179). In any event, the first church in Comfort was a Lutheran Church, which was built in 1892.

The towns of New Braunfels, Fredericksburg, Boerne, and others in the Texas Hill Country between San Antonio and Austin prospered. The population grew, and by 1857 there were 35,000 Germans in Texas and perhaps 25,000 of these were settled in the Hill Country.

The Germans were becoming a potent influence upon the affairs of the state through their political activities and their newspaper publishing. Their first important political organization met in San Antonio on May 14 and 15, 1854. The platform which they adopted at the convention had a plank which declared, "Slavery is an evil, the removal of which is absolutely necessary according to the principles of democracy" (Biesele 198). When this platform was published " . . . a veritable storm broke loose" over the slavery plank, which might be expected (Biesele 199). "That platform placed the entire German population of Texas in a bad light" and thereafter all German Texans were characterized as abolitionists (Biesele 199).

The German Texans began influencing elections by 1859[4] and a reaction to this influence is found in an Anglo-controlled San Antonio newspaper that reported:

> On election day a horde of political lepers crawled to the ballot-box and there nullified the votes of thousands of your countrymen, who had weighed well the principles in controversy. Great God! Shall these things always exist? The unanimity with which the German and Mexican vote was cast against the American candidates [cannot mean] that the thou-

sands and tens of thousands of these ignorant, vicious, besotted greasers who swarm the land, are more capable of self-government than [we are] (Haley 121).

The platform statement in 1854 and the newspaper editorial in 1859 in San Antonio attest to the growing German Texan influence on the eve of the Civil War. It is quite likely that the majority of Anglo Texans held intense and negative views of this minority foreign group as manifested in their reaction to the slave plank and the election outcome. To believe otherwise would be naive. It is likely that this attitude was present at the Nueces River in August 1862.

CHAPTER 9.

DEATH

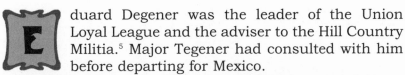duard Degener was the leader of the Union Loyal League and the adviser to the Hill Country Militia.[5] Major Tegener had consulted with him before departing for Mexico.

Degener had two sons who were with Major Tegener in the defensive group on the Nueces River awaiting attack. They were twenty-two-year-old Hilmar and twenty-year-old Hugo. Both boys were born in Brunswhich, Germany, and the family immigrated to near Sisterdale (Kendall County) in 1850. Both boys were messmates of John Sansom; Hugo was a second lieutenant in Jacob Kuechler's Kendall County Company.

As the attack by the Confederates on the Union position developed, Hugo and Hilmar Degener found themselves in the thick of things. They both were wounded.

Lt. Hugo Degener, who was covering the right wing, had his back shattered by two bullets. He crawled to Ernest Cramer's position and bade him farewell. Hilmar Degener was shot in the mouth. Although wounded, the brothers continued to fire their weapons.

Another defender was thirty-two-year-old Wilhelm Telgmann, who also had been born in the same town as the Degener brothers. He was a farmer and he received a body wound during the battle. However, he too continued to fight to the best of his ability.

The acting commander, Amil Schreiner, was killed

Western edge of Unionist camp looking north toward twin peaks of Dutch Mountain in the background. The site has been authenticated through discovery of artifacts.

—Private collection of Paul Burrier

On August 10 the Unionist camp faced this cliff behind Dutch Waterhole.
—Private collection of Paul Burrier

This map shows the location of the battle site. The map is oriented with the north and "Dutch Mountain" at the top. The battle occurred about 150 yards to the west of "Dutch Waterhole" on the West Prong of the Nueces River.

—Adapted by Paul Burrier from U.S. Geological Survey map

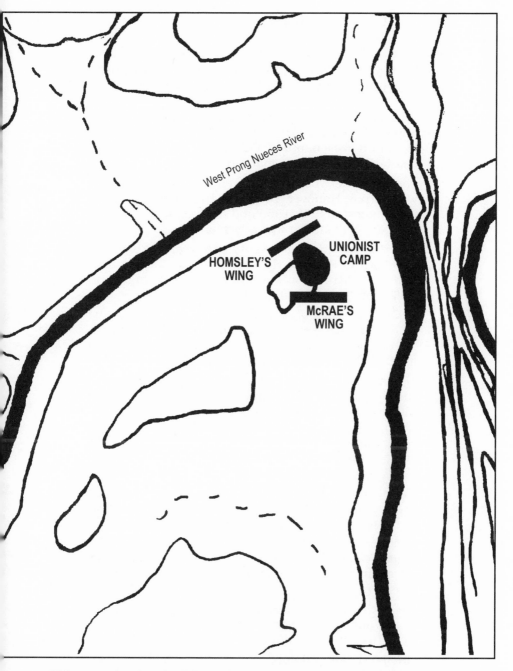

This map is sketched from the map on page 74 and shows the location of the Unionist camp and the two wings of the Confederate force.

—Drawn by Paul Burrier

leading a counterattack. The Mexican, Pablo Diaz, also was killed at the battle site. Twelve other Unionists were killed during the battle, and they are listed below.

Fritz Behrens. Fritz was married to Auguste Vogel and on October 1, 1861; they had a son, Hermann. Hermann was baptized on the day of his father's death. Fritz's widow remarried in 1864.

Louis Boerner. Louis was twenty years of age and was born in Hanover, Germany. His family arrived in the Comfort area in 1855 and he lived with his older brother, William. He was a farmer.

Albert Bruns. He was twenty-four years of age and was born in Prussia. He arrived in the Comfort area in 1854 where he was a farmer. He was single and was another messmate of John Sansom.

John G. Kallenberg. Age nineteen, he was born in the Duchy of Saxe-Weimar in Germany. His mother died in 1850 and the rest of the family immigrated to Texas in 1853. John was a farmer living in his father's home.

Heinrich Markwort. Heinrich, a blacksmith, was thirty-two years of age and was born in Prussia. He married Maria Magdalene Hohmann on April 15, 1855, and they had four children. The last child was Sara Auguste; she was born on August 6, 1862, while her father was traversing the Edwards Plateau. His widow remarried in 1867.

Christian Schaefer. This young man was eighteen years old. His wife, Wilhelmina Kitcher, was pregnant at the time of her husband's death. On February 16, 1863, she gave birth to his son, Christian.

Louis Schierholz. This twenty-nine-year-old man was a teamster, single, and lived in the home of Willam F. Boerner.

Heinrich Steves, Jr. Heinrich was twenty-eight years of age and was a farmer-teamster. Born in Prussia, he arrived in the Comfort area in 1855.

Adolph Vater. Adolph, who lived with his father, August Vater, was twenty-three years old and single. He too was born in Prussia and lived in Gillespie County.

Friedrich (Fritz) Vater. A resident of Gillespie County, he married Christine Heubbam and they had a son and a daughter. The daughter, Henriette Auguste, was born on September 21, 1862, a month after her father's death. His widow remarried in 1863.

Heinrich Weyershausen. He also was a Gillespie County Unionist and was thirty-two years old. He was born in the Duchy of Nassau and was a farmer. Heinrich married Henriette Flick on August 6, 1851. He left two children, ages eight and four. His widow remarried in 1865.

Michael Weirich (Weyrich). This man was born in 1839 in Prussia. He and his parents settled in the Live Oak Creek community in Gillespie County in 1853. He was single and lived with his parents.

At 6:00 A.M. Lieutenant McRae had attacked thirty-nine defenders and over the course of several hours at least nine men were wounded and sixteen men were killed for a total of twenty-five Unionist casualties. This left fourteen men defending the position. Up to this point there had been two Confederate charges. Jacob Kuechler took charge of the survivors, and they agreed to try to repel a third Confederate charge and then attempt an immediate withdrawal to the rear. They did so and retreated down a small creek bed to the surrounding hills. These fourteen men plus the twenty-eight men who had left the camp site between 3:00 A.M. and 6:00 A.M. mostly dispersed into small groups and many of them returned to the Hill Country. There were at least three distinct groups. One group was the twenty-three Germans who left the battle site by the beginning of the battle at 6:00 A.M. They probably split into smaller groups later. The second group was John Sansom with the other four Anglos. The third group consisted of survivors of the Confederate assault who left the battle site mostly in small subgroups.

During the battle, the Confederates had at least two men killed and eighteen wounded. One of the wounded was Lieutenant McRae but it is believed he was still capable of giving commands. Although wounded, he would survive that injury only to die from disease (typhoid fever or yellow fever) on September 10, 1864. One of the commands he may have given was to his junior lieutenant named Lilly. Lt. Edwin Lilly was junior by reason of the date of his rank. Historically the most odious tasks are assigned to junior officers. After the Union survivors had melted into the cedar-brakes, hills, and gullies, there were still wounded Germans on the battlefield that were unable to withdraw. Three of the survivors were Wilhelm Telgmann, Hugo Degener, and Hilmar Degener. It is likely these three men were executed by shooting in the afternoon of August 10; by all reports the executioner was Lieutenant Lilly. As a junior officer, it is inconceivable that he was acting independently. One may assume he was following the orders of Lieutenant McRae or another senior officer.

There were other confirmed wounded Unionists at the battle site, and they are listed below.

> *Henry Kammlah, II.* Henry was born September 8, 1839, in Immensdorf, Braunschweig, Germany. The family arrived in Texas in 1845 and in Gillespie County by 1850. He married Amalie Betz on January 21, 1859, and they had two children at the time of the battle. Although wounded, he escaped, lived a full life, and died on January 26, 1923.

> *Ferdinand Simon.* Ferdinand was born about 1826 in Hessen-Darmstadt, Germany. He was Ernest Cramer's brother-in-law (Cramer was the captain of the Kendall County Company). Although wounded he was mobile, but he was captured near the battle site four days later by one of Lieutenant McRae's patrols. Rather than being executed, he was arrested. He was tried and sentenced to death by hanging by the Confederate Military Commission in October 1862. However, the death sentence was never carried out because martial law was annulled before his planned execution. His case was transferred to the Confederate District Court at Austin for trial but he was never tried. In March 1863 he obtained a writ of habeas corpus for his release but he was not released. He remained in prison for the rest of the war.

William Vater. Vater was seriously wounded during the battle but his Union compatriots hid him prior to their leaving. The Confederates did not find him and he survived his wounds.

Franz Weiss. Franz was nineteen years of age and was born in Prussia. He arrived in the Comfort area in 1855 and worked as a farm laborer. Although wounded, he and his twenty-six-year-old brother, Moritz, were able to make it back to Comfort undetected. The route they and other survivors may have taken was southeast to Uvalde, east to Castroville outside San Antonio, and north toward Boerne or Comfort (Burrier "Notes," 241-2).

Adolphus Zoeller. Although wounded, he returned safely to his home. He was born on December 1, 1839, in Hessen-Darmstadt, Germany, and immigrated to the Sisterdale area. He and his wife, Auguste, had four children.

There were other survivors who fled the scene and were intensely sought by the Confederates. The Confederates apparently had made a decision to eliminate the principal Union leaders, and in particular, to execute any Unionist who had borne arms against Confederate troops. Consequently, there were a number of executions in the summer of 1862 and nine of these, which are discussed below, were of men who had been at the battle site on the Nueces River.

Conrad Bock. Bock was twenty-six years of age and he was born in Prussia. He arrived in Gillespie County about 1854 and married Pauline Flick (age 16) on May 5, 1860. She gave birth to their daughter, Hanchen, on February 20, 1862. Conrad was a member of the "Luckenbach Bushwhackers," a guerrilla group which dealt with the Confederates and their sympathizers. Conrad Bock was captured by a detachment of Duff's Partisan Rangers, which was under the command of Lt. Richard Taylor on August 23, 1862, near Boerne. He was hanged the next day about a mile and a half north of Boerne near Cibolo Creek. His widow remarried in 1864.

This photo, taken on the anniversary of the battle (August 10, 1997), shows at top the small valley where the Unionists withdrew at the conclusion of the battle. Dutch Mountain, to the north, is shown in the background. —Private collection of Paul Burrier

Fritz Tays. Tays was captured along with Conrad Bock. He was born in Hanover, Germany, in 1842 and his father died before 1850. His mother remarried, and by 1850 he was in Texas along with his mother, stepfather, brother, and two sisters. He was a laborer and the family lived near New Braunfels. He was hanged along with Conrad Bock. (According to Paul Burrier in his Notes, page 243, after the Civil War the Kendall County Reconstruction Grand Jury indicted Richard Taylor and James Duff for these executions. However, neither of them were located and therefore they were never tried. The indictments remain open today.)

Herman Flick. Herman was single, a farmer, and a

brother to Conrad Bock's wife, Pauline Flick Bock. He was captured by a Confederate detachment near Medio Creek, an intermittent stream in Medina County. It empties into the Medina River southeast of San Antonio. He was hanged, probably on August 20, 1862.

August Luckenbach. He was said to be one of the leaders of the "Luckenbach Bushwhackers," a militant group which allegedly practiced retaliatory attacks upon Confederate supporters. He may have been wounded in the August 10 Nueces Battle and fled. August was born in 1833 in the Duchy of Nassau. The Luckenbach family came to Texas on the ship *Johann Dethardt* in December 1845. August became a farmer and married Henriette Bertha Goebel about 1858. Two sons were born to them. August Luckenbach was captured by the same detachment that had captured Herman Flick. He was captured on August 20 about eight miles north of San Antonio and was hanged, probably at the same time as Herman Flick. His widow remarried in 1865.

Heinrich Stieler. Heinrich was seventeen years of age when he died. He arrived in the Comfort area in 1856, and was a laborer. He was born in the Duchy of Anhalt. Heinrich was captured by the Confederate army around August 20, 1862, and apparently had nearly convinced his captors that he was on his way to join the Confederate army and had gotten lost. However, about this time Theodore Bruckish (see below) was captured nearby and Stieler's story was not confirmed. Stieler was then executed and his body was left unburied. This incident took place in the vicinity of Kerrville or Comfort.

Theodore Bruckish. Theodore was twenty-four years of age and had emigrated to Texas from Germany by 1860; he settled in the Comfort area early in 1861. His capture by the Confederates followed that of Stieler's (see above). Under questioning he admitted that Stieler and he had been with the Unionist group on the Nueces River on August 10. He was executed under the same circumstances as Stieler.

William F. Boerner. Boerner was born around 1830 in Hanover, Germany, and in 1856 he settled on Cypress Creek near Comfort. He was a farmer and he married Laura Stevens on February 14, 1861, in Kerr County. He too was captured and executed around August 20, 1862. His pregnant wife gave birth to a son after his death.

Adolph Ruebsamen. Adolph and Louis (see below) were brothers. Adolph was born in 1840 in the Duchy of Nassau, and he arrived with his family in Gillespie County by 1850. He may have been a member of the "Luckenbach Bushwhackers" (see above). He was captured along with his brother around August 20, 1862; both of them may have been wounded in the process. He and his brother were executed together.

Louis Ruebsamen. Adolph's younger brother (born in 1843). Both he and his brother were single. Both of them were captured and executed at the same time.

The German community in the Hill Country understandably reacted to these incidents with rage and sorrow. This was especially true in Comfort, where much of the youth of the small community had perished. Early on it was decided this loss would be memorialized. In 1866 a group of citizens went to the battle site to recover the bones of the deceased. The party recovering the remains of these men found that "most of the skulls of the dead men had bullet holes in them" (Sansom, Letter 3). Whether the shorts were inflicted before or after death is inconclusive. None of the men had been buried.

The people in and around Comfort were bitter and forever referred to this incident as a massacre. The Comfort Heritage Foundation, Inc. has called this massacre the "blackest day in the history of the Confederacy and the Civil War" (quoted on page 14, Gazette Edition, *Kerrville Daily Times* n.d.). More expansive hyperbole was found in the Feature Section of the *Dallas Morning News* of May 5, 1929. The headline read: "The Blackest Crime in Texas Warfare." The story went on: "Thus the years have labeled the tragedy of Nueces River where 27 Union soldiers died. For three years the bleaching bones of those young Germans, who left Gillespie County to fight against slavery and were surprised and slaughtered by a group of renegades, lay among thorns and underbrush at the fork of the river" (Ransleben 100 [facing]).

Modern scholarly texts still refer to the Nueces affair with emotionally explosive words. Professor John Duncan of Texas A&M University developed a chronology of important events in Texas and this was updated by B. P. Gallaway (editor) in 1994. An entry in the chronology for August 10, 1862, states, "Sixty-five German Unionists, trying to make their way to Mexico, are attacked near Fort Clark by Captain C. D. McRae of the Second Texas Mounted Rifles and all but twenty of the Germans *savagely slaughtered* [emphasis added]" (Gallaway 248).

Perhaps in the end it makes little difference what descriptive words are attached to this incident because the emotional residue will endure. Most Comfort residents today know about the Nueces River affair and feel sad.

However, there were also numerous men who survived the battle and executions. One of them was Ernest Cramer, who had been in the thick of the battle nearly to the end. There came a point in the battle where he realized they could no longer hold their position. Of the original group, he reports that he, Moritz Weiss, and "Kuhler" were the only ones not wounded. (There is no record of a "Kuhler" being involved in any way with the Nueces affair and it is assumed that he is referring to Capt. Jacob Kuechler). He says, "We decided to withdraw through the thick timber to the other side of the water. We took with us all of those not too badly wounded" (Cramer 4). He adds that this small group went up the valley and met another group of eight survivors. They all journeyed until noon and the wounded could travel no further. They made a shelter for them and went to search for water. Returning to the shelter at 4:00 P.M. they found the wounded gone. The next morning they found water and then later the wounded men, with the exception of Ferdinand Simon, who had been captured by the Confederates. Within a week many of these survivors had reached their home counties. Cramer said he hid in a thicket one-half mile from his home in Comfort because he thought it was too dangerous to go home. He eventually went to nearby Leon Springs and many of the other survivors trickled back to their homes.

Another survivor, August Hoffmann, reported that the heat was insufferable on August 10 at 9:00 A.M. when their position was overrun. He stated that the survivors fled and later he and Mathias Pehl found water. As they were walking along the water's edge they noticed a ripple in the water. "We looked and saw a man sitting under a willow bush in the water with just his nose out of the water." Hoffmann continued, "He raised his head just enough so he could see. When he saw us he said, 'Oh, God, it is you.' It was Adolf Vater" (Letter, n.p.). He had lain there all day and was shot through one arm and the chest. The group took him with them for a distance and then made a comfortable bed for him from cedar branches. The Hoffmann group continued their journey and he says that eventually about fourteen men made it home.

Three other survivors did not attempt the trip home. They were Heinrich Schwethelm, Jacob Kusenberger, and Carl Graff. Schwethelm was twenty-one years old and was born in Prussia. He was a farm laborer. Kusenberger was born in 1834 in the Duchy of Nassau and was a farmer. He was married to Auguste Molzberger on January 4, 1857, and they had three children at the time of the Nueces affair. It is likely that he was a member of the Luckenbach Bushwhackers. Graff also was born in Prussia in 1829 and his occupation was that of a wheel-wright. His wife, Carolina, and their only child were born in Prussia as well.

This trio made for the Rio Grande about fifty miles away and started out on foot. They had no food or water and hid during the day while traveling at night. After the first night's travel they were able to find a water hole. At sunrise on Wednesday August 13, the group reached the

Rio Grande, which they managed to swim across. On the other side a Mexican frontier company took them into custody and gave them the first real food they had eaten since August 9. They went on to Piedras Negras and from there to Matamoros. By October, seventy-six men gathered there and they were shipped in a schooner, chartered by the United States Counsel, to New Orleans, Louisiana, where on October 26, 1862, they enlisted in the First Texas Cavalry, United States Army (Schwethelm 26-29).

Heinrich Schwethelm was a Unionist group member and a survivor of the Battle of the Nueces. Later he was a Union army captain and a Texas Ranger captain.

—Private collection of Paul Burrier

August Hoffman was a Unionist camp member and the last living survivor of the Battle of the Nueces.

CHAPTER 10.

DEGENER'S TRIAL

There were immediate reactions to the armed conflict at the Nueces River. The Confederate Military Commission was meeting in San Antonio that summer, and this commission has been alluded to in the discussion of Ferdinand Simon. Another important figure appeared before the commission. He was Eduard Degener, the leader of the Union Loyal League, the adviser to the Hill Country Militia, and the father of Hugo and Hilmar Degener, who were killed at the battle site. Eduard Degener was arrested and taken to San Antonio by August 26, 1862. He was charged with being "hostile to the Government of the Confederate States, and is a dangerous and seditious person and an enemy to the government of the Confederate States" (Burrier "Notes" 352). Specifically he was charged with having knowledge of the Hill Country Militia, making slanderous and seditious statements against the Confederacy, and assisting and arming the militia.

The trial opened on September 27, 1862, and one of the witnesses for Degener was Ernst Altgelt, one of the founders of Comfort. He was most helpful in Degener's cause. Altgelt testified that in July 1862 he had spoken with the Degener boys and advised them to take the oath to the Confederacy. Eduard Degener at the same time urged his sons to take the oath, he explained. Further he testified that Eduard was not at the organizational meeting of the militia and that he believed the father was neutral, neither Unionist nor Secessionist. Another witness testified that the Degener boys were headstrong and their father could not control them. This witness said that when Germans began resisting the Confederates, the father had advised his sons to have nothing to do with them. Further, the father had no notion his sons were going to Mexico until one-half hour before they left, according to this witness. This witness also said Degener was a good citizen and obeyed the laws of the state. Another witness told of Degener advising people to take the oath. Charles Beseler, the older brother of Ernst Beseler who was killed at the battle site, also testified for Degener. He spoke of occasions on which Degener had advised his sons to stay at home and obey the law.

In any event the evidence presented on behalf of the head of the Union Loyal League was overwhelming. Surprisingly, Degener was only ordered to post a $5,000 bond to ensure that he would conduct himself as a loyal citizen of the Confederacy.

CHAPTER 11.

THE RIO GRANDE

J acob Kuechler was persistent. After returning from the battle at the Nueces River, he decided to try once more to get to Mexico. He organized a group of approximately seventeen men to make the trip. This group included some of the survivors of the Nueces River affair, including Maj. Fritz Tegener, who had recovered from his wounds. It also included some men who had not been at the Nueces engagement. The group departed in October 1862 and took nearly the same route the August group had taken. They were mounted and well armed and revisited the Nueces River battle site, where they built a stone pyramid over the bones of their fallen comrades.

Confederate authorities again became aware of their flight and General Bee dispatched Company K, 32nd Texas Cavalry to intercept them. Capt. Stokley M. Holmes commanded this group. He had organized this cavalry company in Caldwell County, and it became a Confederate unit in February 1862.

The Confederates located the Union group on the Rio Grande near Del Rio on October 18, 1862. On reaching the ford in the river, the Unionists drew Confederate fire and attempted to cross the Rio Grande while firing back. The Germans took heavy losses and eight men died. These eight men are listed below.

Peter Bonnet. Peter was born at Charlettenberg, Prussia, on February 8, 1833, and the family settled in Texas in 1845. As he was crossing the Rio Grande, Peter was shot in the body below the shoulder. Others dragged him across the river to the opposite shore. However, Peter died from his wounds on March 12, 1863, at Piedras Negras, Mexico.

Joseph Elstner. Joseph was about twenty-two years of age and arrived in the Comfort area in December 1861. He was a farmer and had been with the Unionist group at the Nueces River. He was either killed by Confederate fire or drowned.

Ernst Felsing. He was born in 1829 in Hessen-Darmstad, was single, and was a farmer. He arrived in the Comfort area in 1854 and was one of the Unionists at the Nueces River in August. He too either drowned or was killed by gunfire.

Henry Hermann. Henry was born in 1841 in the Duchy of Nassau, and he lived with his parents. He had been with the Unionists on the Nueces. He too was shot or drowned as he tried to cross the river.

Valentine Hohmann. Hohmann was born in 1829 in Saxony and was a laborer and farmer. He was married and had six children and had been with the Germans at the Nueces River. He was killed in a similar fashion as he tried to cross the Rio Grande. His widow was pregnant and gave birth to their son on Christmas Day 1862.

Fritz Lange. Fritz was a stonemason who was born in 1832 in Hanover. He arrived in Texas in 1851 and settled on Verde Creek in Kerr County. He drowned or was hit by gunfire while trying to cross the river.[6]

Franz Weiss. Age nineteen, Franz was wounded in the Nueces River battle and survived only to die after being shot in the water at the Rio Grande.

Moritz Weiss. Age twenty-six, and Franz's older brother, he drowned while trying to help his brother. Both of them had been members of the Luckenbach Bushwhackers.

Confirmed survivors who had been wounded include the following:

> *Sylvester Kleck.* Kleck was born in Hohenzoeller, Prussia, and was seventeen years of age. He lived with his parents and was a member of the Luckenbach Bushwhackers. He was one of the Germans at the Nueces River. He arrived in Gillespie County by 1850. While in the Rio Grande he received several gunshot wounds to his body, grabbed the tail of his horse, and was dragged to the Mexican side of the river. He was nursed back to health in Piedras Negras, Mexico, by a fifteen-year-old Mexican girl named Juanita. They later married.
>
> *Maj. Fritz Tegener* was again seriously wounded at the Rio Grande as he had been while commanding his troops at the Nueces River battle. He made it to Mexico, where he remained for the rest of the Civil War.
>
> *Capt. Jacob Kuechler* was the leader of the Rio Grande group and had been in charge of a company at the Nueces River engagement. He too was wounded in the Rio Grande and his wounds prevented him from enlisting in the Union army. He too stayed in Mexico for the rest of the war.

To summarize, a total of thirty-six men, who were loyal supporters of the Union, died for their beliefs, either at the Nueces River battle or in related activities shortly thereafter. The account here is but a sampling of many men who died in Texas for their beliefs. This type of activity was not isolated to the Hill Country.

The summer of 1862 was a particularly deadly time throughout Texas because the Confederate authorities were terribly threatened by the armed rebellion that had developed. The issuance of orders for martial law was the beginning of an effort to systematically suppress the rebellion. This, in turn, led to viciousness on both sides; producing murders, property destruction, and the like.

Between May 1862 and March 1863, the Hill Country

Militia and its individual members were the objects of destruction by elements of James Duff's Partisan Ranger Company. Confederate sympathizers were the targets of destruction by members of the Hill Country Militia or by the Luckenbach Bushwhackers. This war within a war was in full force that hot summer of 1862.

There were many examples of killing. There was a similar incident only a week before the October 18 ambush on the Rio Grande by Capt. Stokley M. Holmes. Around October 11, 1862, a Union group trying to get to Mexico had been attacked on the Rio Grande near Eagle Pass. Twenty of the twenty-two men in the group, who were referred to as Dutchmen and Bushwhackers, were said to have been killed by Capt. Thomas Rabb's Company A of the Frontier Regiment.

Another incident occurred sometime between July 20 and August 22, 1862, when a detachment of James Duff's Partisan Rangers is said to have captured and executed four Kerr County residents. They were Ephrian Sebird Henderson, Gustaf Tegener (Fritz Tegener's brother), Frank Scott, and Hiram Nelson (Sansom "German Citizens were Loyal to the Union" 12; Sansom "Account Book Ledger Sheet" 29). Howard Henderson confirms this in his 1908 letter to John Sansom that says in part,

> . . . I know that J. W. Duff and his company of murderers killed many of my neighbors and friends. My uncle and cousins, Schram Henderson, my wife's father and brother, Turknette, were murdered, my neighbors, Hiram Nelson, Frank Scott and his father, Parson Johnson and old man Scott were all butchered by Duff and his gang. Rocks were tied to their feet and they were thrown in Spring Creek (Ransleben, 119)[7]

Another major incident occurred in northern Texas in the same month as the Rio Grande ambush. A Union Loyal League was formed in Gainesville, Texas, near the Oklahoma border in June 1861. It was formed about the same time as the Hill Country Union Loyal League and with the similar purpose of passively supporting the Union cause. After introduction of the Confederate Conscription Act, its purpose changed to one of resisting the draft and maintaining a spy system for the army of the North. Members of the League, who were drafted into the Southern militia, planned to meet an invasion by the Federal army and then desert to the approaching army.

In October 1862 word of this movement got out to the populace which reacted with terror because of their fear of an armed rebellion. Undoubtedly, the people in Gainesville were aware of the Nueces River battle, and this may have fueled a state of hysteria. Martial law was declared and the hysterical populace captured and hanged twenty-five Unionists without benefit of a trial. Fifty more were arrested and forty of them were hanged after a trial (Buenger 86-87). Once again Union loyalists had died for their beliefs.

In fact, viciousness against Union sympathizers was reaching epidemic proportions in Texas as it was in some other Southern states. In his memoirs John Sansom mentions two men who were especially cruel. One was Maj. John Henry Brown, who was from Belton, Bell County, Texas. Brown was said to have been backed by the Knights of the Golden Circle, and he hunted down men who refused to be conscripted into the CSA Army. He sent his scouts into Blanco County to find nine men who were in hiding there and eventually eight of them were killed. In Travis County, Brown's soldiers arrested three brothers, William, Gid, and Frank Wilises. The soldiers then ". . . took them to the State Capitol, and hung them in open daylight to a Live-Oak tree in sight of the Governors Mansion" (Sansom "Memoirs" n.p.).

The other man mentioned by Sansom was Maj. J. W. D. Alexander. Alexander, who was a member of the Knights of the Golden Circle, had been made a major by Governor Lubbock. Nearly a year after the Nueces affair, eight men were on their way to Mexico. Major Alexander and twenty-five of his men took out after them and found the group resting under a tree near Castroville in Medina

County. Major Alexander placed the eight men under arrest. They were tied onto their horses and taken to Bandera County. Two miles outside the town of Bandera, on July 25, 1863, the men were put to death. Seven of them were hanged and one was shot in the chest. The eight men named are C. J. Sawyer, W. M. Sawyer, George Thayne, Jack Wetmore, Jack Kyle, John Smart, N. Van Winkler, and William Shumake. Sansom added, "The massacre of Union men began under Lubbock's administration and was continued to the close of the Civil War in Texas, 1865" ("Memoirs" n.p.).

On occasion, this viciousness did become "civilized" when circumstances turned the participants toward a military commission or a court of law. The results were sometimes ludicrous. As mentioned earlier, after the Nueces River affair, Eduard Degener, the head of the Union Loyal League and adviser to the Hill Country Militia, was arrested and brought to trial before the Confederate Military Commission in San Antonio. He professed his innocence and convinced the commission he knew nothing of the league or the militia. Although found guilty of minor charges, he was ordered to post a $5,000 bond and to obey the laws of the Confederacy.

The point is that brutality was commonplace throughout Texas during that hot summer. Such brutality was not isolated to Texas, however. Every state in the South had its share of loyalists and some of these states raised units for the Union army. Friction and hate were, of course, ordinary between secessionists and Unionists in both the North and the South but these emotions were more intense in the Southern states, where Union loyalists were in abundance. Not only in Texas, but elsewhere, Confederates so feared Unionists that brutal tactics were commonly used to suppress them. Such tactics occurred in numerous locations throughout the South and these "little wars" were never very civilized. During an era when armies sometimes made grand gestures of magnanimity, viciousness characterized contacts between individual secessionists and loyalists.

PART TWO

ANALYSIS

CHAPTER 12

THE NUEEES RIVER AFFAIR AND THE TIMES

It is necessary to view the Nueces River incident within the context of what was happening at the time. Anglo Texans had mistrusted Germans from the time of their arrival in the Hill Country. Most Germans were intensely anti-slavery and most Anglo Texans were intensely pro-slavery. This issue caused divisiveness within Texas as it did in other states and the nation. Texas seceded from the Union, but there was not unanimity in this action. Passions began to boil over. Armed guerrilla bands had been active near the Nueces River for years prior to the affair. In Missouri there was rioting which led to the deaths of soldiers and civilians. Finally, the Civil War erupted in states near Texas in three separate battles over a one-month period. Shiloh was a huge battle in which more soldiers died than in the three previous wars the U.S. had fought (Revolutionary War, War of 1812, and the Mexican War). Death was becoming commonplace.

In 1862, German citizens from Comfort, Texas, and the surrounding area were killed as they were trying to escape this turmoil. At the same time, others of them intended to join the Union army. Nevertheless, these Texans sacrificed

their lives for principles in which they strongly believed—
individual freedom and loyalty to the Union.

This affair has been labeled as a massacre and others
refer to it as a battle. There are elements of both "massacre"
and "battle" in this "affair." A massacre, by definition, is a
killing of a number of usually helpless or unresisting
human beings. A massacre is nearly identical to murder,
which pertains to unlawfully killing a person especially
with malice aforethought. For those who describe the
Nueces River affair as a massacre, clearly the prisoners,
some of whom were executed after the firefight, became victims of a massacre or murder. Of that there can be little
question. Consideration of the rest of the activities associated with the affair may lead to different conclusions.

By definition, a battle is fighting between organized
bodies of individuals who are armed and trained for regular or irregular warfare. Pursuing for 100 miles a fleeing
armed force, which is trying to reach a neutral country,
suggests elements of retribution. But this affair cannot
simply be dismissed as retribution because Confederate
Gen. H. P. Bee had issued a legitimate order. What causes
difficulty here is trying to understand the interpretation
and execution of the order.

The key part of his order was that the Germans who
refused to take the oath of allegiance were to ". . . be treated
summarily [promptly] as traitors in arms." This suggests
that there are two kinds of traitors: those who are armed
and those who are unarmed. There had been established
in Houston a military commission whose purpose was to
try "all cases of seditious and traitorous persons against
whom charges are preferred" (OR Ser. 2, Vol. 4, 857). A
similar commission began meeting in San Antonio on July
2, 1862 (Burrier "Notes" 327). No reference is made to the
unarmed versus the armed traitors, but the Germans certainly could be considered as "seditious and traitorous"
for their activities, and they could have been arrested on
these charges. However, it appears that Lieutenant McRae
had no intention of arresting these armed German
Unionists. He had the opportunity before launching his

attack at sunrise to offer surrender to the Germans, should they wish to capitulate. However, it is unlikely they would have done so because of their justified fear of execution. It is probable that Lieutenant McRae knew whom he was pursuing since the Germans had been watched closely since the militia was formed. Most likely he understood his orders were not to encourage arrest.

It is reasonable to conclude that Lieutenant McRae interpreted his orders as requiring him to destroy this enemy force. By this date in the Civil War nearly all military people on both sides had concluded that war is killing—that is what war is all about. General Bee perceived these armed insurgents as a military threat, and he concluded that this threat needed to be eliminated. They were not to be treated as traitors, but as traitors in arms, and this suggests there were to be no prisoners. However, his orders were ambiguous on this point and did not specify that the insurgents were to be arrested and brought to trial or killed.

In his planned attack, Lieutenant McRae practiced classic military maneuvers of the day as he prepared for a battle. All of the Germans had the opportunity to avoid a pitched battle should they wish to do so. They had three hours between the first firing and the sunrise attack to flee under the cover of darkness. Thirty-nine Germans decided to defend their position, and thus a battle developed. Consequently it is proper to characterize this part of the affair as a "battle" rather than a "massacre."

If this is a battle, however, then the Confederates, at its conclusion, found on their hands a number of prisoners of war. To these POWs the Confederates did not extend the normal and humane treatment usually afforded prisoners by both sides. Instead they executed them. This is where elements of retribution begin substituting for civilized behavior. Unfortunately, it was not the first time nor the last time that prisoners were executed during war. This is not said to condone. The execution constitutes criminal behavior, and this is where the word "massacre" properly fits.

Another factor needs to be considered, however. In many countries treason is considered an offense which can be punishable by death, but such punishment usually follows a trial. A Confederate Military Commission was in session in San Antonio from July 2 to October 19, 1862, and one of the battle survivors, Ferdinand Simon, appeared before them in October 1862. He was found guilty and was sentenced to death, but the sentence was suspended. He spent the rest of the war in prison (Burrier "Bio" n.p.). As an aside, it should be mentioned that General Bee wrote that the McRae group did their work effectively. He made no mention of the fact that there were no captives. Lieutenant McRae had indicated earlier there were no prisoners due to the stout resistance of the Germans. McRae and the other officers were later promoted, and this fact suggests that the absence of prisoners met with General Bee's approval.

There are those who would indicate that the battle casualty figures suggest a massacre. At the conclusion of the morning assault, the German group had sixteen people killed and nine wounded for a total of twenty-five casualties. The casualty rate was sixty-four percent. In his battle report Lieutenant McRae reports he had a total of two killed and eighteen wounded (OR Ser. 1, Vol. 9, 616). Some of his men (perhaps four) were noncombatants because they were holding horses, so their casualty rate was about twenty-two percent. The Union side had a casualty rate nearly three times that of the Confederate side. Furthermore, at the end of the battle the Unionists had eight times the number of men killed as did the Confederates. On the surface these figures would seem to suggest a massacre, but these data require further examination.

Four strategic and tactical decisions on both sides led to these disparate figures. First, Lieutenant McRae had identified the group he was following, and had a good idea of the size of the opposing force through his informants and from reading the signs on the trail. Major Tegener probably had no idea a hostile group was following him since he apparently did not employ scouts at the front, rear, or sides to detect any approach. A prudent commander would have done so in this era. On August 9 it was suggested to him that his unit was being followed and he dismissed the possibility. He did not send troops out to investigate the stranger who was seen on a nearby hill, and he took no unusual steps with nightfall coming, such as increasing the size of the guard.

Second, when McRae discovered the campsite, he made a careful reconnaissance of the encampment to develop a viable strategic plan before attacking what he assumed to be a formidable force. Major Tegener did not have the opportunity to develop a strategic plan because the presence of the McRae group at his campsite was a surprise.

Third, and of crucial importance, the Unionists, after the death of the two guards, decided to reduce their defending force from sixty-seven to thirty-nine men, without having any idea of the size of the opposing force. Furthermore, Major Tegener made the tactical error of setting up a defensive position in topography that was unsuitable for such a position. It was open ground with cover nearby, which would conceal the attacking force. He had ample opportunity before the attack to locate a more suitable position nearby.

On the other hand, the Confederates developed a good tactical plan. Lieutenant McRae initiated the attack with the classic double envelopment maneuver that was commonly used during these years. This enabled him to attack the flanks of the enemy while concentrating his firepower upon a single target, and it forced Major Tegener to disperse his firepower in two directions.

After the guards detected him, Lieutenant McRae resisted the temptation of launching a night attack in favor of waiting for daylight so he could better coordinate his force. He was unfamiliar with the ground on which the fighting would take place and did not know what preparations the enemy was making. Taking these factors into consideration, it was a wise decision by McRae to delay the assault. It is noted that the dawn attack no longer had all the components of an ambush because some elements of surprise had been compromised. The guards had discovered the presence of the hostile troops before the main assault was made. However, there were still elements of uncertainty for the Germans. For example, they had no idea of the size or armament of the attacking force or any knowledge of the tactics they might employ. The Confederates, although discovered, continued to remain concealed prior to assaulting the German position. Thus, some elements of an ambush continued to be present.

Fourth, the Confederate force had better armament than did the Union force. The Unionists were armed with muzzle-loading rifles, and they were in an open position. This is pertinent because it is necessary for a soldier to partially expose his anatomy when loading this weapon between shots. The Confederates, on the other hand, were equipped with Sharps breech-loading rifles (or carbines), which are more accurate and do not require the soldier to expose his body while reloading. Furthermore, the rate of fire of the Sharps rifle is greater than the muzzle-loading weapon.[8] Boatner states that the weapon was accurate up to 600 yards and he adds that "At 300 yards a 24-inch pattern could be made with 20 shots. A rate of up to 10 rounds per minute could be achieved, which was three times as fast as the muzzle-loader could be fired" (735-36).

All of these factors in combination help to explain the relatively high losses in the Tegener group. The high casualty and death rates among the Unionists were due to sound strategic and tactical decisions being made by the Confederates. In turn, these decisions were skillfully executed. In hindsight, Major Tegener made some relatively poor military decisions, and one could speculate that these decisions were generated by emotions rather than by rational military thought. This was a proud, perhaps stubborn group of Germans, who were a cohesive unit with the courage to become martyrs. This was a hard-fought battle, not a massacre. The suspected subsequent execution of three wounded prisoners was murder as was the execution of those caught as they were trying to return to their homes.

Regarding the battle at the Rio Grande in October, the Confederate force, this time, apparently had the element of surprise in its favor and caught the Unionists in the river as they were trying to cross. It is noted that the Union group took the same route they had intended on their first trip when they were stopped at the Nueces. This may have worked in favor of the Confederates in terms of launching a surprise attack. This engagement was more of an ambush as opposed to a pitched battle. Nearly three-quarters of the Germans were casualties due to the accurate fire of the Confederates and their superior position on the land. No prisoners were taken. The Confederates were carrying out the same mission as they had at the Nueces, and once again they completed their mission efficiently.

Portions of the Nueces River affair were a battle and portions were a massacre. The Rio Grande affair was an ambush. The word "affair" is used to describe these incidents because it does not carry an implication of judgement, and because that word was often used in official military correspondence. It is not such a value-laden word as "massacre" and "murder." However, beyond the killing of these men there are broad Confederate policy and strategy concerns to consider.

A month after the affair on the Nueces River, Gen. Paul Hebert probably had dismissed the matter from his mind in order to deal with other important matters. But this Confederate general, a former U.S. Regular Army officer, knew how to obey a direct order from a superior. He was about to get one.

Correspondence dated September 12, 1862, from Richmond, Virginia, came across his desk from General Cooper of the Adjutant and Inspector General's Office. But what caught General Hebert's eye was that General Cooper was speaking on behalf of Confederate President Jefferson Davis. It isn't every day that the president comments on a directive a general has issued. The correspondence stated:

General: Your proclamation extending martial law of
the State of Texas has been laid before the
President, and is disapproved by him as an unwar-
rantable assumption of authority and as containing
abuses against even a proper administration of martial law.

He went on to quote from General Orders No. 66 and
56 that stated in part:

. . . military commanders have no authority to sus-
pend the writ of habeas corpus, all proclamations of
martial law by general officers and others assuming
a power vested only in the President are hereby
annulled (OR Ser. 1, Vol. 9, 735- 36).

This was "a slap in the face" to General Hebert. He
knew that he had only done what Gen. Earl Van Dorn had
done when he assumed command of the Trans-
Mississippi Department in January 1862. General Van
Dorn had imposed martial law in portions of Louisiana
and Mississippi, but the governor of Louisiana had objected. General Hebert decided to defend himself by getting support from Texas Governor Francis Lubbock. In his
letter to General Hebert, Governor Lubbock advocated the
continuance of martial law because of the "fact of there
being many disloyal people in various localities of the
State, whose vile tongues and bad example is held in
check by the effect of martial law." The governor further
spoke of his extensive borders, which were "enabling disloyal and timid men to escape the country, thereby avoiding all the responsibility of citizens . . . I can but hope that
martial law will be kept in force . . . by which the country
will be kept quiet and our citizens required to remain at
home and perform such duties as may be demanded of
them by the Government of our choice" (OR Ser. 1, Vol.
53, 830).

General Hebert wrote to General Cooper from San
Antonio on October 11, 1862—a week before eight
Germans were killed at the Rio Grande and perhaps before

Captain Holmes was dispatched to intercept them. In this correspondence he reported that in obedience to the order dated September 12, "I have revoked my proclamation extending martial law over the State of Texas and all orders based upon it." He then went on to defend his implementation of martial law and stated that he had no choice but to issue the proclamation "to prevent traitors from leaving the country and congregating beyond the frontier, and there to plot mischief to our Government . . ." (OR Ser. 1, Vol. 53, 829). Finally he appended Governor Lubbock's letter to support his defense.

Martial law as imposed in Texas was somewhat broader than is usual. In the conventional sense, martial law refers to law administered by military forces when the civilian law enforcement agencies are unable to maintain public order and safety. Habeas corpus refers to the issuance of a document to bring an imprisoned person before a court or judge to guard against illegal imprisonment.

The evidence suggests that Texas authorities used martial law not to maintain public order and safety. Instead it was used to try to minimize evasion of conscription into the Confederate military, to prevent dissidents from leaving the state and joining the Union military, and to enforce loyalty to the Confederacy. Too often martial law was used as an instrument to sanction excesses against those politically incorrect citizens who were disloyal to the Confederacy regardless of whether or not they took any direct action to support the Union. A number of citizens were arrested for their political beliefs, and there is little evidence that the military authorities honored any writ of habeas corpus.

Texas was understandably angry with its citizens who were disloyal to the Confederacy and especially so with the Hill Country Germans who were most outspoken and perhaps overbearing about the subject. Consequently these persons were targeted for correction. The trouble for the Texas government and the Confederacy was that what they set forth to accomplish was impossible to achieve, and this increased their level of frustration. They found it impossible to coerce loyalty to the Confederacy. They found it impossible to seal the borders to prevent citizens from fleeing conscription and joining the Union army. They nevertheless expended huge and scarce resources of men and material to try to accomplish these aims with little success. The Rio Grande border in particular was a magnet which attracted the Germans to Mexico, and the Texas authorities had no more success in sealing that border than we have today. Furthermore, habeas corpus was considered merely a formality of law that could be readily dismissed in practice. These policies were doomed to failure because they could not be enforced; they were unjust, unreasonable, and probably illegal.

At the beginning of his administration, President Jefferson Davis declared martial law in areas that were in danger of attack by Union forces and he suspended the writ of habeas corpus. Accordingly, martial law was declared in Richmond, Virginia. The reason that President Davis prohibited Hebert's use of martial law was that the Confederate Congress had given President Davis (and the president alone) only limited scope in imposing martial law. It eventually forbade him entirely from suspending the writ of habeas corpus. In a states' rights environment, several Southern governors (especially those from Louisiana and Mississippi) had objected to the Confederate government imposing such restrictions on their citizens. The CSA government early on began to accept its limitations in terms of coercing loyalty and limiting the rights of the citizens of its states. For example, it found it did not have the necessary military resources to keep the citizens of western Virginia from forming a new state and joining the Union. The Confederacy found it would have to live with these inconveniences and fight the war as best it could.

On the other side, President Abraham Lincoln was able to use suspension of the writ of habeas corpus to effectively deal with dissidents. He suspended the writ to preserve public safety. Chief Justice Roger B. Taney of the U.S. Supreme Court said the president did not have that authority under the Constitution, and consequently the U.S. Congress, in August 1861, legalized Lincoln's suspension of the writ. This gave Union military officials the power to arrest those aiding the Confederacy and to detain them indefinitely. This power was widely utilized. McPherson stated, "Suspension of the writ was a vital weapon against rebellion" (289). A strong central government approach in the North versus the strong states' rights sentiment in the South enabled the Union to maintain better control over its dissidents (largely in occupied territory) than was the case in the Confederacy. Many of those arrested in the North and in occupied territories were released later after taking an oath of allegiance to the Union.

The contrasts between the administration of martial law and the application of habeas corpus in the North and South were marked. In the North, martial law and suspension of the writ of habeas corpus were used extensively to silence political foes and to minimize hostile action by secessionists. However, prison sentences were generally imposed and political enemies frequently were released after they signed a loyalty oath. Execution of secessionists and political foes was a rarity.

In Texas, martial law was utilized for similar purposes but was expanded to try to keep Northern sympathizers within the state. A prison sentence was not common and the writ of habeas corpus, although not suspended, was seldom honored for the few in jail.

In contrast to the North, the Texas German dissident was much more likely to be executed than imprisoned. There were several reasons for this. One was that Texas authorities became obsessed with the notion of attaining internal security and conformity. Although this is common in war, especially civil war, this quest for security reached greater heights in Texas than was the case in the Union, this in spite of the fact that the North had the problem of overseeing hostile populations in captured territories.

A second reason was that, unlike the North, the South,

either consciously or unconsciously, equated disloyalty of the Unionists with treason. The crux of the problem here was that the Germans felt that if they were loyal to the Confederacy they were being untrue to their original vow of allegiance to the United States. The Confederates could not accept this and saw being disloyal as being treasonous, and treason is a capital offense in many countries. Treason is, of course, the overt act of attempting to overthrow the government. While the German may have been seditious in his resistance to the authority of the Confederate and Texas governments, he seldom actively tried to overthrow that government. Instead he tried to escape the controls of that government. Nevertheless, German and Anglo Unionists were commonly viewed as treasonous people who deserved to be killed.

There is little question that members of the Union Loyal League and the Hill Country Militia were deemed to be disloyal by the Confederacy, but these disloyal citizens were much more likely to be executed than was the case in the North. Disloyal persons in the North were subject to General Orders, No. 30 that stated:

> All persons not in the military service, who shall be convicted of disloyal expressions, oral, written, or printed, favoring the rebellion, shall be punished therefore by fine [assessment] or imprisonment, or both, or by being sent beyond the lines, by sentence of a military commission (OR Ser. 1, Vol. 22, pt. 2 239).

While the loyalty oath began to move Texas Germans from neutrality to passive resistance or acquiescence, it was the conscription law that propelled them to aggressive action. It was one thing to take an oath but quite another matter to be forced to leave your family and to bear arms against a nation to whom you are loyal. By the spring of 1862, the South had a desperate need for military manpower and on April 16, 1862, the CSA Congress enacted the first conscription law in the history of America, "The Enrollment Act." This law declared that all able-bodied white male citizens between the ages of eighteen and thirty-five were liable for three years of military service (the upper age limit was raised to forty-five in September 1862). The law as amended had many exemptions, however. A drafted man could hire a substitute for himself; categories of employees (such as Confederate and state civil officials, teachers, apothecaries, railroad and river workers, and others) were specifically exempt; and one white man on every plantation that had twenty or more slaves was exempt. The Enrollment Act was probably the most unpopular act that the Confederate government passed. A draft act in the North was also unpopular, but not to the extent that it was in the South. There were a number of reasons for this.

Most Southerners believed in a voluntary military force, and felt that forcing men to serve in the military was a demeaning act. Conscription was seen as an unwarranted extension of the power of the central government, and an action that interfered with the traditional rights of the states to conduct their own affairs. Some even contended that it was unconstitutional because it usurped the rights reserved by the states.

The various exemptions were particularly onerous because they were liable to manipulation or fraud. The substitution exemption favored the man who had sufficient wealth with which to hire a substitute, and it was the most controversial exemption. Its existence gave rise to the common saying, "A rich man's war but a poor man's fight." This exemption was so unpopular that it was repealed in December 1863. The exemption for categories of employees came to be widely abused. Governors who opposed conscription hired many new civil servants that became exempt. Apothecary schools and teacher training schools sprang up, and men signed up to become eligible for exemption. Last, the "Twenty-Negro Law," which was designed to keep the white overseer on the plantation, was widely resented because it granted a privilege to a class of people on plantations which constituted only about five percent of the Southern white population.

This military draft proved so unpopular that many men in the South (who otherwise may have been supportive of the Confederacy) took to the woods or swamps to avoid military service (as did the Germans in Texas). This especially was the case in the Appalachian Mountain chain, where "uplanders" responded to the draft with a mass exodus into the forests to avoid contact with the enrollment officers. In time, the enrollment officers came to avoid these hideouts for fear of death, since the disaffected groups became quite large and aggressive. The South was unwilling to spare military units to try to get these disaffected groups under control and many of them either avoided the draft throughout the war or joined Union army volunteer groups. It is important to note here that these Southern men were not hunted down and killed by any organized units because there was not the will or the available military power to deal with them. This is in contrast to the Texas Germans, who were hunted down and killed for their failure to obey the draft law. One difference here is that the German group was much smaller and was easier to catch when it left the hills and was found on open ground.

CHAPTER 13.

OTHER SOUTHERN LOYALISTS

A t the outset it needs to be understood that "the solid South" was *not* the solid South. The "Myth of the Lost Cause" affirms that there was a solid confederacy of Southern people who stood firm against the tyranny of the North. In fact there never was unanimity in the South; there never was a "solid South." There was a divided South, and this divisiveness was nurtured by a strong states' rights environment. From the beginning, division haunted the South. Throughout the South people who lived in the Appalachian highlands generally were pro-Union, whereas people of the plantation areas generally were pro-secession. The plantation area people were the fire-eaters of the Confederacy and controlled the political life of the state. The "uplanders" tended to be pro-Union and did not have the political power to impose their will upon the state. The plantation people possessed political clout, and through their influence states were guided toward secession and war.

There are numerous and dramatic examples of this division in the South. Texas, as previously noted, found a significant minority of its citizens voting to stay in the Union, which was the case in most Southern states. In

Texas, many of the Hill Country counties voted against secession, but the vote against secession was even more dramatic in Tennessee. There "the voters of mountainous East Tennessee cast seventy percent of their ballots against secession" (McPherson 283). In fact the mountain area in western Virginia and eastern Tennessee was a hotbed of Unionism which led to the creation of the state of West Virginia and to "little wars" and guerrilla activity in the Tennessee Appalachians.

These events were typical of what was occurring throughout the South from 1861 to 1865. "Bloody Kansas" was especially notorious for the undeclared war that existed near the Missouri border. Rampaging gangs of thugs, bent on revenge, murder, robbery, and pillage, roamed the countryside under the guise of patriotism and ideology. Across the border in Missouri, loosely organized guerrilla bands became training grounds for the outlaw gangs that would rule the countryside after the war. This is where Jesse James got his education. Sometimes these gangs or guerrilla groups in Kansas and Missouri would be attached to Confederate army commands to disrupt Union supply lines.

Michael A. Vasile describes these types of guerrilla units when he says:

> Composed mainly of local residents rather than reg-
> ular troops, these men emerged as a criminal ele-
> ment which struck terror in the hearts of soldier
> and citizen alike. The character of these guerrillas
> was ideally suited for the type of war that was
> fought on the western frontier. They were rugged,
> individualistic, unsavory in character and were all
> too often aspiring to the profession of blood and
> booty (11).

In the east, these guerrilla wars were fought on a larger scale. In the western counties of Virginia there had been longstanding sentiment for separate statehood. These mountaineers felt they had little in common with the planters of the lowlands, and Virginia's secession accelerated their desire for separation. The electors in the west voted against secession by a three-to-one margin on October 24, 1861, and West Virginia attained statehood on May 23, 1862. However, statehood would not have been attained had it not been for the presence of a large Union army in that region which Robert E. Lee found he could not dislodge.

But it was in Tennessee that conflict was most acrimonious between Confederate sympathizers and Union loyalists. Eastern Tennessee was heavily populated with Unionists. Union loyalists began lobbying the Lincoln government to intervene militarily in East Tennessee, or assist by supplying the insurrectionists with money and arms for guerrilla activities so that Confederate supply lines might be harassed. At the same time, many of these loyalists flocked into Kentucky to join the Union army and frequently engaged in skirmishes with Confederate troops trying to deter them in their quest.

Meanwhile, President Lincoln was trying to get military assistance to eastern Tennessee as he had done in western Virginia. He called on Gen. Don Carlos Buell to come to the aid of the dissidents in eastern Tennessee, but Buell had his own problems blocking the advance of Gen. Braxton Bragg's troops into Kentucky. Fighting there had begun on May 26, 1861, and was concluded by October 6, 1861. Lincoln wanted Buell to move immediately to East Tennessee to support the insurgent Unionists, but a cautious Buell contended he could not supply his troops on so long a march. He declined to invade Tennessee, saying that advance was impracticable. Lincoln replaced him because of his timidity. But it was too late and because of the lack of a Union army in East Tennessee, the Unionists there were not to enjoy the success of their brothers in arms in western Virginia.

The Nueces River-Rio Grande affairs were concluded by mid-October 1862. At about the same time, a group of Union loyalists raided Marshall, North Carolina, and thirteen of the alleged participants later were executed without a trial. These incidents occurred in isolation of one another, but each event was similar and loosely connected with the other. In a sense the Nueces and Marshall events were a microcosm of the American Civil War and were but two of many such events which occurred throughout the South. These have often been referred to as minor events but, of course, they are not minor if one has lived or died through the event. Indeed they are part of a larger fabric which has been referred to as "the war within the war." Examining this fabric will put "Nueces" within a larger context that may serve to illuminate why the Nueces affair occurred and may give insight into the ramifications of this incident.

By November 1861 an insurrection against the Confederate government had been organized in East Tennessee and this culminated in the burning of five railway bridges. The Confederate government moved to suppress this rebellion in December 1861. Secretary of War Judah P. Benjamin[9] allegedly instructed that bridge burners were to be caught and hanged with their bodies to be left hanging in the vicinity of the burned bridges. These instructions were carried out, and this barbarity was justified by President Davis' proclamation that all those not in allegiance to the CSA should leave the state before October 1861.

This was but the beginning of guerrilla war in eastern Tennessee, and it was to accelerate. This activity spilled over into western North Carolina, where the guerrillas would take refuge in the mountains on the border between the two states. Guerrillas and draft dodgers began pillaging and looting in western and central North Carolina, and the citizens of that state understandably reacted with alarm at the apparent impotence of the Confederate government to do anything about it.

This set the scene for an event that was similar to the Nueces River affair. In the fall of 1862, a group of perhaps fifty Unionist guerrillas from Laurel Creek, Madison County, North Carolina, struck the town of Marshall, North Carolina, which is north of Asheville and near the Tennessee border. Their apparent objective in Marshall was to obtain a supply of salt, which was in short supply due to the war. Salt was used to preserve food, in the absence of ice, for an army on the move. Plundering followed, and it is probable that a revenge motive was involved. There had been a long-standing feud between these men from Laurel Creek and elements of the 64th North Carolina Regiment under the command of Col. L. M. Allen. Some of the men in the guerrilla group were deserters from Colonel Allen's regiment, and Allen's home in Marshall was plundered (OR Ser. 1, Vol. 26, 854).

The Confederates sent a detachment from the 64th North Carolina Regiment under the command of Lt. Col. J. A. Keith to Laurel Creek, and he took prisoners (none of whom resisted) from their homes. Four prisoners were jailed. Thirteen prisoners, ranging in age from fourteen to fifty-six years of age, were taken by the soldiers to a secluded place, where they were made to kneel down and were executed by shooting (OR Ser. 2, Vol. 5, 836). Eight of the thirteen probably had not been involved in the raid on Marshall. They were shot on suspicion of their involvement in this and other raids. These killings probably were driven by a desire for reprisal.

North Carolina Governor Zebulon B. Vance was incensed when he learned of these events. Before learning of the executions, he had written to Confederate General Henry Heth[10] in Knoxville and said, "I hope you will not relax until the Tories [Unionists] are crushed. But do not let our excited people deal too harshly with these misguided men. Please have the captured delivered to the proper authorities for trial" (OR Ser. 1, Vol. 26, 854). After learning of the executions, the governor wrote Brig. Gen. William G. M. Davis in Knoxville and expressed his chagrin concerning ". . . such cruel and barbarous conduct . . ." (OR Ser. 2, Vol. 5, 839). Governor Vance also wrote to James A. Seddon, secretary of war, and said, "I desire you to have proceedings instituted at once against this officer [Keith], who if the half be true is a disgrace to the service and to North Carolina" (OR Ser. 2, Vol. 5, 841). The secretary of war directed Gen. Daniel Smith Donelson in Knoxville to investigate.

In May 1863 Secretary Seddon advised Governor Vance that an examining board had found Lieutenant Colonel Keith to be incompetent, and his resignation was accepted. At the hearing Keith told the board that his commanding general (Heth) had instructed him to kill any prisoners. General Heth told the board that he had instructed Keith that those found to be armed were not to be treated as prisoners of war in the event of any engagement with them. General Heth added that he authorized no "maltreatment of prisoners who have been accepted as such . . ." (OR Ser. 2, Vol. 5, 956). Upon learning that J. A. Keith had become a civilian, Governor Vance stated, "Murder is a crime against the common law in this State and he is now subject to that law" (OR Ser. 2, Vol. 5, 952). This is where the matter ended.

The American Civil War was not civil. No war is. The Civil War is also misnamed since such a war is between opposing groups of citizens of the same country. Since the South established the Confederate States of America (a new country), the war properly has been named the War of the Rebellion. A rebellion is an open, armed, and usually unsuccessful resistance to, or defiance of, an established government. On the other hand, if the rebellion is successful and leads to a change of government, it becomes a revolution, as in our revolution of 1776. All of this is said to put the Nueces River affair within a larger perspective rather than to isolate it from parallel events.

What then were the repercussions, similarities, and differences between the raid by Unionists on Marshall, North Carolina, and the Nueces River affair in Texas?

One similarity is that the men in both Texas and North Carolina were loyal to the Union. The Texas men were members of the Union Loyal League. The North Carolina men, who earlier had sent a representative to the Lincoln administration to seek assistance in resisting the CSA, were probably receiving some direction from Washington. Men in both states died because of commitment to their loyalties and beliefs, and they died at the hands of Confederate military forces. These two Union groups were acting independently of a command structure while the Southern troops were following orders, as they understood them, from their military commanders. The Texas cavalry unit was under the direction of the District of the Rio Grande, while the North Carolina unit was under the command of the Department of East Tennessee.

A major difference between the Texas and North Carolina Unionists lay in the type of activities in which they were engaged. The Texas Unionists, for the most part, passively resisted the Confederate government, engaged in no serious insurrectionist activities, and served to a limited degree in an information gathering capacity for the Union. They engaged in no aggressive armed activity, but were armed to protect themselves. They engaged in a firefight only when fired upon. On the other hand, the North Carolina group had every intent to overthrow the Confederate government if possible, and it was regularly engaged in plundering, theft, burning railroad bridges, damaging property, and stealing salt.

The North Carolina Unionists frequently were referred to as a guerrilla organization, and that probably is an accurate description. Dr. Francis Lieber was an authority in 1862 on guerrilla warfare and he stated, ". . . a guerrilla party means an irregular band of armed men, carrying on an irregular war. . . . The irregularity of the guerrilla party consists in its origin, for it is either self-constituted or constituted by the call of single individual" (OR Ser. 3, Vol. 2, 301-309). He added that the group is disconnected from the army (although it may be attached to an army group from time to time) insofar as pay and provisions are concerned. Consequently, theft of supplies and food was common for guerrilla groups so that they might sustain themselves in the field. Further, the guerrilla group is irregular as to its permanence since it may be disbanded and called together from time to time. (See also Michael A. Vasile's description of guerrilla activity in the West on pages 159-60).

If one accepts this descriptive activity of a guerrilla

group, it is fair and accurate to characterize the North Carolina loyalists as guerrillas. However, it does not adequately describe the Texas Union Loyal League militia, for it was more defensive and passive in nature. The militia was in existence to avoid the military draft in Texas, to wait for the arrival of the Union army at which time it would join with that group, and to protect Unionists from death or plunder by Confederates or their sympathizers. The Hill Country Militia did not have the desire or the means to attempt an overthrow of the Confederate government. It did not systematically attempt to destroy Confederate property, to disrupt lines of communication, to kill CSA soldiers, to steal CSA supplies, and the like. These things that they did *not* do would be exactly the things one would expect guerrillas *would* do.

So, if the Union Loyal League Hill Country Militia was not a guerrilla group, what was it? One member, Ernst Beseler, certainly became a "bushwhacker" and assassin when he killed Basil Stewart. However, that was a solo action, although the group sanctioned it. Would one of the following labels be suitable for this militia?

- Freebooter or privateer (an armed robber)
- Brigand (a detached soldier who commits robbery)
- Partisan (a designated body detached from the main army)
- Spy (an intelligence gathering activity)
- Rebel (a person who resists authority and control)

The first three labels are not descriptive of the Hill Country Militia. One might be inclined to characterize the German Texan as a spy, but the trouble here is that espionage was practiced infrequently, and any intelligence gathered was of little use to the Union. The only label that fits well is that of rebel, but that serves to place both German Texans and Confederate Texans in the same pot. Yet, German Texans were rebelling against Confederate controls just as the Confederate Texans were rebelling against United States controls.

The Texas Unionists died while trying to escape these controls. The North Carolina Unionists died for actively attacking the Confederate government by plunder, property destruction, and disruption of lines of communication and supply. It is ironic that the Texas Unionists died in the process of escaping while eight of the thirteen North Carolina Unionists died for a raid in which they did not participate.

The reaction of civil authorities to the death of civilians in their state is instructive. The North Carolina governor was incensed that some citizens of his state had been shot without benefit of a trial. He made inquiries to top military authorities and to the secretary of war. Finally, he seriously considered having J. A. Keith tried in a civilian court for murder. Contrarily, the Texas civil authorities reacted differently to the death of German citizens. For the most part there was no reaction on the authorities' part, and they were content to let the military deal with the matter. Interestingly, the military contended that since the Germans were armed they were not to be treated by the laws of war as prisoners of war. Instead they were characterized as armed traitors, and this was used as justification for their execution. At the same time, the armed rebels of the CSA usually were treated as prisoners of war when captured by United States forces during or after a battle. In August 1862 General-in-Chief U.S. Army, H. W. Halleck stated, "The rebel authorities claim the right to send men, in the garb of peaceful citizens, to waylay and attack our troops . . . and to destroy property and persons within our lines. They demand that such persons be treated as ordinary belligerents, and that when captured they have extended to them the same rights as other prisoners of war . . ." (OR Ser. 3, Vol. 2, 301). Apparently the South wanted their guerrillas to be treated as prisoners of war but did not intend to treat Northerners, whom they perceived to be guerrillas, in like fashion. In all fairness, policies on how to deal with guerrillas were in a state of flux on both sides.

The German rebels who were captured were summarily

executed because they had been armed. Had they been unarmed would their lives have been spared? Had they not been German "foreigners," would appropriate civil authorities have pursued the death of these Texas citizens? Nobody knows, and it is pure speculation to follow this line.

Another contrast is the varied reaction of military authorities to the activities of their subordinates. In North Carolina, Lieutenant Colonel Keith was found to be incompetent and was forced to resign from the CSA military. In Texas, Lieutenant McRae's commanding officer stated that the lieutenant carried out his work effectively. Later McRae was promoted.

What is certain is that there were numerous such events during the war. There was brutality on both sides, and this is characteristic of all wars up to the present time. Each event was similar but was shaped by the cultural framework in which it occurred. Civilians often bear the brunt of some brutality in wartime. Witness not only the United States Civil War but also the deaths associated with the Crusades, the elimination of Jews in Germany, the Iraqi treatment of Kurds, and the civilian executions in Bosnia.

CHAPTER 14.

THE ROOTS OF HATE

T he year 1862 in America was a time of turbulence. Many young men in Union and Confederate uniforms were dying on the battlefields. Feelings about the issue of slavery were intense. Civilians were not strangers to bloodshed over slavery and secession, and in some states there were individual instances of a civilian on one side of the issue killing a civilian on the opposing side. This was a violent era. However, there are few recorded instances of American citizens peacefully leaving a hostile environment for the safety of a neutral country, being pursued by a military group, and then being killed for their moral stance on an issue.

The incident near the Nueces River in August 1862 was an extraordinary affair—an event that exceeded the bounds of civility normally found in the Civil War era. The Hill Country Militia rarely took any overt, aggressive action against the Confederate authorities except in response to Confederate provocation. They did not actively advocate overthrow of the Confederate government, but only hoped to support a Union army when it invaded Texas. Instead, their role was that of passively resisting the Confederate loyalty oath and the draft into the CSA Army. The Germans were fleeing to Mexico, where they hoped to express their opposition to the Confederacy by joining the Union army.

A Confederate force pursued the Germans for one week and 100 miles with one nefarious purpose: death. The Confederates did not intend to take prisoners and turn them over to the proper authorities on charges of treason or sedition. Their plan was to annihilate the group. Upon surrounding the Germans, the pursuers gave them no opportunity to surrender in the three hours preceding the attack. After capturing some of them, the Confederates gave them no opportunity to live. Their superiors approved of this action by reviewing the incident favorably in the Official Record and awarding promotions. Currently this might be classified as a war crime.

The emotions that drove the Texas Confederates toward this drastic action were anger and frustration. The anger arose from the refusal of the Germans to conform to the values of the majority. The frustration arose from the policies the Confederacy developed to deal with its dissident citizens. They relied upon martial law and suspension of writ of habeas corpus to try and impose Confederate loyalty upon Unionist Germans. President Davis and the Confederate Congress denied them even these tools after the Nueces River affair. They also tried to seal the Mexican border to prevent the Unionists from fleeing there, but that was an impossible task. These policy decisions failed and produced an increasing level of anger and frustration.

These feelings were not the only ingredients in the recipe for disaster on the Nueces. Another component was hate; it was this that drove the Confederates to eliminate the dissidents. An intense dislike of someone or some group does not develop overnight. It blossoms over time and is incubated by a multiplicity of factors and events. The hatred underlying the Nueces River affair arose from the following factors that are discussed in turn:

- Violence as a way of life
- Slavery as an institution
- Religion as a divisive force
- Politics as a source of polarization
- Cultural factors serving to agitate
- Xenophobia and nativism feeding paranoia

VIOLENCE AS A WAY OF LIFE

Our history reveals us to be a violent people. In the several hundred years before we first came to America, our mother country was frequently at war with France and Spain, and had been engaged in a civil war (Wars of the Roses). She had been a principal in the Hundred Years War (the longest war in history) during the fourteenth and fifteenth centuries. People were hanged or beheaded, imprisoned without just cause, and often treated unjustly under the Elizabethan Poor Laws. Violence was common.

America imported from Great Britain the notion of retaliation. This concept held that if wrong is done to us, then we must directly punish the wrongdoer himself, and thereby restore order and justice. This suggested that we were to act independently and were to be free of external influence and controls (the role of government was narrowly circumscribed). This tradition of retributive folk justice had been carried from the British borderlands to the thinly settled rural areas of America.

These ideas evolved in the American backcountry, where order keeping was accomplished by "regulators" or "vigilantes" who often dispensed quick and violent justice. Vigilante movements began in the eighteenth century in the rural South and later became common in the posse of the southwestern frontier that embraced and perfected "lynch law." This ethic of violence continued to be demonstrated in the form of ambushes, border raids, and border wars in the first sixty years of the nineteenth century in Texas. The central themes of this backcountry social arrangement were violent retribution for wrong done and autonomy of the individual in safeguarding his own interests. It was this systematization of retributive justice that helped create the climate of violence that is ingrained in our culture today.

In the one hundred years in America before the Civil War, our forefathers were engaged in three other wars. Violence was commonplace on our frontier as we expanded into Indian country, and our frontier society was relatively lawless and untamed. Fifteen years before the Nueces River affair, we temporarily ended border disputes with Mexico after a two-year war. These clashes continued after the Mexican War because the land struggles had not been fully resolved. Sometimes these skirmishes or battles were about issues related to the Civil War, and sometimes they were about land, property, or pro-Mexican and anti-Texan sentiments. However, they all contributed to a climate in which killing became a favored method of resolving disputes. We accepted into our mores the notion that violence was a preferred way of dealing with disagreement and that compromise and negotiation were of lesser value.

The notion of the acceptability of physical force produced a climate in which unruly mobs could participate in marauding, property destruction, and killing such as occurred throughout the Texas Hill Country in 1862. During that period many Anglo Texans viewed the Germans, particularly the radical freethinkers, as arrogant and officious, and they became subject to victimization by a group where mob psychology prevailed. This was similar to the group behavior that was portrayed by Walter Van Tilburg Clark in his classic novel *The Ox-Bow Incident*, where a group of men hang innocent men. This same mind-set and acceptability of violence by a clique played a part in the Nueces River affair.

Two pre-Civil War events relating to slavery were characterized by unmitigated savagery. One was the Nat Turner rebellion. Turner was a slave who, in 1831, led a bloody insurrection in Southampton, Virginia. He had become convinced that he had been anointed to lead his fellow slaves out of bondage. The goal of the Turner uprising was to take a nearby arsenal and arm the slaves who would join the rebellion. In turn, the slaves would gain freedom through their armed might. In the process of this rebellion the slaves killed fifty-five white people. At the home of farmer Waller they butchered and decapitated a woman and ten children. The farmers armed themselves, and in a pitched battle they overpowered the slaves who fled. What followed was widespread killing of both innocent, and not so innocent, slaves. Eventually Nat Turner was hunted down and hanged.

Less than thirty years later, a second episode of similar physical force occurred when John Brown, an abolitionist from Kansas, invaded the southern Appalachians to free the slaves. He planned on taking an arsenal and arming the slaves who would join him in the uprising. On October 16, 1859, he captured the U.S. Armory at Harpers Ferry, Virginia. The next night, the U.S. Marines stormed the building the Brown group was defending. This rebellion ended with the capture of John Brown and he was hanged six weeks later.

The John Brown and Nat Turner uprisings were similar because in both instances violence and murder were deemed to be an acceptable method of dealing with what was viewed as a social evil. They also were similar because in both events the leaders were executed by hanging. Many Anglo Texans had migrated from the South and East, and the John Brown-Nat Turner incidents were well known to these men and other Texas citizens. Both episodes were insurrectionist in nature and aimed to free the slave who, it was assumed, would strike back at the master in payment for past wrongs. This real fear of an insurrection in Texas, possibly leading to freeing the slave and putting the white man in harm's way, always lurked in the mind of the white Anglo Texan. All of these factors were in play as precursors to the Nueces River affair.

The Germans were no strangers to violence, and often they had been on the receiving end. Since 1517 they had been involved in religious wars, one of which wiped out half the population (the Thirty Years War). Barbarism was linked to serfdom since the disobedient serf was subject to various harsh punishments and sometimes death. Wars continued to swirl in and around Germany during the Napoleonic era that concluded only about thirty years before the large migration to Texas. One of the reasons for this migration was to escape the residual effects of these wars. Another reason was to escape repressive measures against those who were fomenting and participating in the 1848 revolution in Germany. Many Germans chose to isolate themselves in the Texas Hill Country to try and live in relative peace. For the most part they did so after the Treaty of San Saba River was signed with the Comanches in 1847.[11]

Civility in the United States in pre-Civil War days had broken down over the issue of slavery as is evidenced by the Brown and Turner rebellions. After April 1861 the Union and the CSA were attempting to resolve the issue through use of force. By combining this war mentality with the decline of civility, and with the breakdown of law on the frontier, there was created a volatile climate in which a spark was enough for a deadly explosion. Such a climate existed in 1861 Missouri, where riots erupted and death resulted; the same was true at the Nueces River. Germans figured prominently in both episodes. In St. Louis poorly trained and disciplined German troops panicked when attacked, and killed civilians. At the Nueces River, Anglo Texans hunted down and killed German Texans because they were trying to escape to Mexico. In both instances slavery and insurrection were in the background.

SLAVERY AS AN INSTITUTION

Another important cause of hatred was slavery itself. Slavery had been a part of the United States prior to its founding. During the creation of our Constitution the founding fathers sidestepped the issue by ignoring it. The problem was so divisive that this seminal document would have been voted down had it mentioned slavery. Helotry grew in the South because it was necessary for the development and maintenance of the agricultural and economic systems. In the North there was a great Protestant revival, which led to opposition to bondage.

The greatest threat to America as a Union at mid-century was conflict between the North and South over slavery. It was clear there was going to be a showdown in spite of short-term efforts to try to mollify both sides through legal maneuvering such as the Missouri Compromise of 1820, and the Kansas-Nebraska Act of 1854. The Missouri Compromise excluded slavery north of thirty-six degrees thirty minutes latitude except in Missouri. The Kansas-Nebraska Act repealed this ban on slavery north of the Missouri Compromise line, and provided that the people of the new territories (not the Federal government) could decide if their territories would permit slavery. It was assumed that the territory of Kansas, west of Missouri, would vote for slavery. Consequently, the expansion of slavery north of "thirty-six-thirty" and to the west was a fait accompli. This loosed a storm in our nation. In 1845 Texas had been admitted to the Union as a slave state. This fact, coupled with the Kansas matter, upset the balance of power between the slave states and the free states. This gave birth to the Northern-dominated Republican party and stimulated Northern militancy.

In the first half of the nineteenth century, slavery became such a heated issue that people could seldom discuss it in rational terms. It was an emotional issue on which both sides became increasingly polarized; they inhabited hardening positions from which compromise was impossible. The Nat Turner-John Brown rebellions helped to further cast in concrete these polarized positions. For example, in 1860 the North nearly canonized John Brown for his attempt to free slaves while the South viewed him as a man who would have slaves rise up and kill white people. The slavery issue escalated the hatred one individual might feel for another person who disagreed with his position. Sometimes these feelings expanded beyond the narrow issue of helotism to encompass preservation of a way of life. This enmity produced a powerful determination in the North to preserve the Union, and in the South to secede from the Union and declare loyalty to a confederation of Southern states. All of these elements were present at the Nueces River on that fateful day.

Texas seceded from the Union in 1861 and became one of the Confederate States of America. German Texans found themselves to be a clear minority in a pro-slavery state because they were against bondage. There were many reasons why they took this position. The Germans had come from a background of serfdom, where their ancestors had been subject to the will of the feudal lord. The German peasants in 1525 rebelled against this system when they requested they not be held as property, and asked to be set free. The nobility crushed this effort. Although the feudal system in Europe began disintegrating by the fifteenth century, remnants remained, and the laborer worked under oppressive conditions with little hope of improving his lot in life. This exploitation took the form of unjust taxation and poor working conditions. In eighteenth- and nineteenth-century Europe, movements were afoot for the freedom of man from the stranglehold of the monarchy. The Protestant Reformation and the Age of Enlightenment had aroused the passion for freedom of the individual.

Given the background of serfdom that existed in feudal society, and the fact that the worker was essentially a vassal in the early nineteenth century, it is not surprising that the Germans emigrated in order to seek freedom and something better than helotism. In their new country, Germans hoped to own their own land and work for themselves; they loathed the idea of one man owning another man. Consequently, most Texas Germans were strong slavery opponents in the midst of a state that had seceded from the Union rather than give up slavery. To the Germans such a system was a moral evil. Olmsted observed that the German "was happy in the possession of freedom, undebilitated by mastership or slaveship"

(185). A German is asked why he is in Texas rather than Germany and he replies, "'Because here I am free. In Germany I cannot say at all how I shall be governed'" (Olmsted 185).

On the other hand, the Anglo Texan, who had migrated from the Deep South and had developed cotton farms in East Texas, was as intense in his support of slavery as the German was in opposing it. Helotry had been a way of life for him and his ancestors. The Anglo Texan had come to Texas from states where owning slaves had been the foundation of the economic system since before the founding of our nation. King Cotton thrived in this plantation system. The institution was imported to East Texas and emulated the system found in nearby Mississippi and Alabama. Cotton production would not have been economically feasible without the slave. For the plantation owner the black man was property for which he had paid dearly and he felt he took good care of that property. Also, for him the "freedom of man" argument was specious because the slave was property, not a man. Furthermore, he had a Supreme Court case (the Dred Scott decision) to endorse this position. Finally, if slavery should collapse, a socioeconomic system and a way of life also would collapse.

The Southern non-slaveholder supported the system too because of the economic ripple effect of the plantation. For example, a dry goods store might exist in a nearby town to supply products to the plantation, and this created jobs. Additionally, the non-slaveholding white Southerner enjoyed the benefits of white supremacy. The system of bondage enabled him to occupy a higher social position than that occupied by the black man. No matter what his character, intelligence, or wealth, he was always in a position superior to that of the Negro simply by reason of the color of his skin. Further, a freed slave might compete with him (for example, as a farmer). These economic and social benefits presented many strong motives in the mind of the Southerner to support such a system. He found the anti-slavery view of the German Texan to be intolerable, just as the German found the Anglo's position to be equally reprehensible. It is no surprise that passions ran high in the Lone Star State on the slavery issue. To make matters worse, a number of Southern whites in Texas had a tradition of prejudice against different ethnic groups, such as Mexicans and Indians. Germans may have been the objects of similar prejudice. It was not popular, and perhaps downright dangerous, for the minority Germans to openly proclaim an anti-slavery stance.

RELIGION AS A DIVISIVE FORCE

Organized religion played a prominent role in the events leading to the Civil War, and in hardening the attitudes of people in the South and North so that resolution of conflicts by means other than warfare became impossible. Religion was a unifying influence beginning with the founding of this nation, and in the eighteenth century the Baptists and Methodists of the South did not openly support slavery. Around the beginning of the nineteenth century, the institution of servitude became more firmly entrenched in the South, and the Southern clergy responded by proclaiming that the issue was a matter to be dealt with by civil authorities, rather than by religious authorities. Meanwhile, in the North the churches became increasingly influenced by the rhetoric of abolitionists and took a strong anti-slavery stance.

Gradually the church in the South began changing. Religious revivals produced a more evangelical approach among the Protestant churches, particularly the Baptists and Methodists. These two faiths replaced the Church of England as the predominate denomination.

By the 1830s the Southern pulpit had become ". . . a primary instrument in the defense of slavery as an institution ordained of God" (Chesebrough 144). This came about for many reasons, but one important event was the 1831 Nat Turner uprising. The effect of the rebellion was that the frightened and angry white people, who feared that they themselves might become the victims of a black uprising, strengthened their control over slaves and vigorously defended their restrictive practices. Additionally, Southern institutionalized religion began discussing the idea that if order and regulation of the slave were not increased, there was the possibility that mob rule and anarchy would result, and that something similar to the French Revolution might occur. The definition of "mob" became enlarged to include not only slaves, but also atheists and communists. Thus the German citizens of the Comfort, Texas, area—many of whom were communists and atheists—came to be thought of as a group needing to be controlled.

Nationally, religion began promoting and encouraging a widening gap between those sections of the country above and below the Mason-Dixon Line. Both the South and North felt that God endorsed their differing positions on slavery, and that they were engaged in a holy struggle. In fact, religion played a significant role in leading the South toward secession and into the Civil War.

Religion, by example, was a role model for secession of Southern states from the Union. The majority of Protestant Southerners were Baptists or Methodists, and ruptures over slavery took place within both of these denominations at about the same time. In 1843 the Methodists split over slavery. Pro-slavery Southerners withdrew from the denomination and formed the Methodist Episcopal Church a year later. In 1845 the Baptists split over slavery along sectional lines, and the pro-slavery Baptists formed the Southern Baptist Convention. These activities helped to propel the Southern states toward secession, and the pulpit found biblical support for that secession.

Previously, religion had been a unifying force in this nation, but the slavery issue served to fracture our national unity. The ruptures of organized religion polarized our society and served as a model of how to deal organizationally with the rift caused by slavery. The religious model was one of splitting "that old time religion" into smaller units reflecting sectional interests. Thus, religion contributed to our becoming a divided society and legitimizing the concept of withdrawal or separation from a larger group.

A dominant belief in this period was that God guided the affairs of individuals, states, and nations. Because of this belief, both sides felt that God sanctioned their respective positions, and once again the pulpit found scriptural support for these positions. Confederate nationalism drew its imagery, its language, and its themes from evangelical Christianity. For example, Confederate ideology often portrayed Southern people as God's chosen people, and much of the South saw the Civil War as a holy war which was ordained by God. On July 7, 1861, the Episcopal Bishop of Texas tied together patriotism and religion when he declared that ". . . in all of history there had never been a higher or more noble duty than the one to which the South was now called" (Chesebrough 221). Another Southern preacher, J. W. Tucker, on May 16, 1862, said from the pulpit,

> Our cause is sacred. It should ever be so in the eyes of all true men of the South . . . . Soldiers of the South, be firm, be courageous, be brave; be faithful to your God, your country and yourselves . . . . Your cause is the cause of God, of Christ, of humanity (Chesebrough 236).

The Southern preacher, reflecting the views of his congregation, indicated that the South had the Bible on its side while the Northern people were infidels. German Texans did not share these views.

There were other sources of religious friction between the Anglo Texans and the German Texans. One reason Germans had migrated to Texas was to escape religious persecution. During and after the Protestant Reformation they became enmeshed in the crossfire of the struggle for their souls by the Protestant and Roman Catholic churches. The two branches of Christianity fought over a number of issues. Martin Luther challenged traditional religious doctrines, many people followed him, and the

Lutheran Church was created. But in the end, it was still the ruler in each German state who had the right to choose Catholicism or Lutheranism and then impose his choice on his people. By the 1840s communism was gaining favor, and it fostered atheism or agnosticism. German citizens chaffed under the religious choices imposed upon them by their rulers and they immigrated to Texas, where they hoped to establish their own religious practices without interference by the state. The Catholic and Lutheran churches became the dominant religions in the Texas Hill Country. In Comfort, the choice was made to avoid formal practice of any organized religion. Due to the influence of the freethinkers, there were no churches in Comfort until 1892, although services may have been held in homes.

The religious preference of the Anglo Texan, who frequently was an English-Scotch-Irish Protestant who had migrated from the southern or southeastern United States, was often Baptist or Methodist. These denominations frequently conducted their services in an emotional and evangelical manner that was quite different from the German religious service. Services of the German Lutherans and Catholics were performed with a good deal of formality and ritual, and almost always in Latin (Catholic Church) or German (Lutheran Church). Church music also was different. The Baptist Church sang hymns that often were based on folk tunes from Appalachia America; the Catholic Church maintained liturgy and music taken from deep European roots; and the Lutheran Church usually sang hymns that were based on music written by the great German composers.

Some Protestants were suspicious of what was taking place in the German churches and thought the strange language of the services was perhaps an evil plot. This developing paranoia may have been the basis for unfounded rumors in 1861 and 1862 that the Germans were planning an insurrection to free the slaves and take over Texas. The Germans looked upon Protestant services as bordering on irreverence, and as being unsuitable to properly worship the Lord. In short, the German Texan and the Anglo Texan were relatively intolerant of the way each practiced his religion, and this constituted another source of friction, mistrust, and enmity. On a national scale this angst was exacerbated by the divisive stance taken by organized religion on the issues of secession and slavery, and by the conviction of the churches in the North and South that each of their causes was just and was ordained by God.

POLITICS AS A SOURCE OF POLARIZATION

The Anglo Texan and the German Texan almost always were far apart on political issues. Germans tended to support the anti-slavery Republican Party and Anglos tended to vote pro-slavery Democratic. They mirrored the classic political schism that existed across the country in 1860.

The two groups had distinctly different ideas on how government should be organized. The Anglo Texans supported a system where the role of the Federal government was limited and the role of the states was emphasized. The German Texans favored a strong central government.

The Anglo Texan came out of a political system where the states attempted to maintain control of the Federal government. For years Southern state delegations had heavily influenced Federal congressional activities. In the late 1840s the Southern-controlled Congress tried to expand the territory where slavery might be introduced. Northern states reacted, and by 1850 the balance of power had begun shifting so that the North gained control of Congress. The South emphasized the importance of a strict interpretation of the Constitutional guarantee of states' rights, and this stance was fundamental to its political behavior. The Southern dominated Democratic platform supported slavery and emphasized states' rights (which limited the role of the Federal government). These political issues led Texas to secession in 1861 and to membership in a confederation of Southern states where individual states parsimoniously handed some of their power to the Confederation.[12] The 1861 secession of Texas from the United States of America was not a new event for these citizens since they had exercised the practice a quarter of a century earlier when they rebelled against Mexico.

The Germans, on the other hand, were the products of a culture in which there was strong control at the local level by nobility. They had grown up in a system where there was a loose organization of individual kingdoms ruled by an autocrat. The German Texans disliked this system because it was the source of much of their oppression. They were interested in moving toward a strong central government that was directed by a constitution written by and for the people. The Germans revered the United States Constitution, with its strong concept of unification, and they had difficulty conceiving why anyone would want to remove himself from such an arrangement. Secession was a foreign concept to them. Consequently, German Texans supported a strong central government in this country, and they endorsed all efforts to strengthen the Union. They were opposed to the concept of states' rights, slavery, and secession; these issues likewise were opposed by the Republican Party. So the German Texans became strong supporters of first, Sam Houston, then Abraham Lincoln, and finally the Republican Party.

There was continuous political friction between the Democratic Anglo Texans and the Republican German Texans. The discord was intense and frequently would erupt into name-calling. The Germans would become the "God damn Dutchmen" or "Black Republicans," and the Anglos would become the "Amerikanas." This friction and divisiveness was a constant irritant in the lives of both groups, and contributed to growing animosity.

CULTURAL FACTORS SERVING TO AGITATE

There were other factors that exacerbated the divisiveness between the German Texan and the Anglo Texan. First and foremost was language. The Anglo spoke English, of course. The German may have been bilingual, but he preferred speaking in his own language. Some academic

Germans would speak Latin. Most activities in the community were carried out using the German language, and this would include reading and singing.[13] The Anglo Texan could not understand these languages and frequently suspected that they were used as a means for planning subversive activities. This view of a foreign language is not unlike the attitude today of some people who oppose a foreign tongue being spoken in the workplace and support "English only" legislation. The German Texan who understood English often had difficulty comprehending the colloquialisms, dialects, and twangs in the speech patterns of the Anglo Texan.

Germans tended to reside in communities where other Germans resided. The German communities generally were isolated from Anglo communities by reason of geographical features, and by the tendency of the Hill Country Germans to avoid assimilation into the Anglo culture. Naturally, they were more comfortable with their own people and they tended to stay within those cultural boundaries. Of necessity, they were involved in self-help societies because such groups enhanced survival skills in their new country. However, this and other practices further isolated them from the Anglo. This isolation may have caused the Germans to appear to be aloof.

The German Texans and the Anglo Texans were strangers to one another, and their contrasting ways of life were discussed by Lich, who stated,

> . . . the German newcomers were generally better educated and more widely read than their American counterparts; they were tradition-bound and preferred their old ways to the new. To them, the Americans were . . . rambunctious and often vulgar. The Germans tended therefore to remain silent and apart from their countrymen . . . (75).

Even the music enjoyed by the two groups contributed to dissension. The Germans enjoyed their native folk tunes and the music of German classical composers. The Anglos enjoyed the folk tunes of the Appalachian hills and the Carolina lowlands. It was difficult for one to hear the music of the other with any sense of enjoyment or acceptance.

One group of Germans in the Hill Country completely mystified the Anglo Texan. These were the freethinkers— the radicals, the intelligentsia—who gathered in the "Latin communities" and participated in Latin language debates late into the night. The Anglo Texan could not understand how anyone could live in a commune where property belonged to all and where atheism could be practiced freely and openly. This group was viewed with suspicion and was watched closely by the Anglo Texan. These radicals, mostly from the Comfort area, were heavily represented at the Nueces River incident.

Further, the German Texan usually was a good and productive farmer who was efficient and well organized. His success in his farming operation was accomplished without the use of slaves. Some of the Anglos were less successful in their farming even with the use of slaves. This alarmed the Anglo, whose anxiety served as another source of friction. All of these cultural factors led to the isolation of one group from the other and contributed to misunderstandings, poor communication, mutual suspicion, and enmity.

XENOPHOBIA AND NATIVISM FEEDING PARANOIA

Germans were the victims of xenophobia, which is the irrational fear of foreigners or strangers, or anything foreign or strange. Closely connected to xenophobia is bias and prejudice, which often is found where minorities hold values different from those of the majority. These all became intertwined and created problems for the Germans because the usual response of the majority was to suppress and isolate the minority.

As a nation, we often have displayed these characteristics when exposed to a "foreign minority." The examples are abundant from the beginning of our nation. After we no longer needed the Native American to survive, we conquered him, relegated him to reservations, and viewed him as a "savage." Later we defined the man with dark skin as property, not a human being; we defined white men of Irish descent as drunken hooligans; we viewed the Mexican as "lazy"; and in our speech, when negotiating a good price on merchandise, we said, "I jewed him down."

The German similarly was feared and despised simply because he was not born in this country, and because he held values different from those of the majority. He faced prejudice and bias, as have other cultural groups in this nation. In response, and partially as a defense mechanism, he formed communities that were isolated from the mainstream. Here he could maintain his culture while sheltering himself from the venom of hate groups. At the same time, however, he deprived himself of opportunities to assimilate the majority culture. This has been a natural response of other minority groups (blacks, Mexicans, Italians, and Jews) in our nation. To a lesser degree it has caused them problems as well. The isolation of the German minority served to exacerbate tensions with the Anglo Texan because the German seldom became known as an individual—a person with the same desires and wishes as any other human being. These conditions are a nurturing ground for xenophobia.

However, such fear is only a partial explanation for the hate and mistrust of Germans, not only in Texas, but also throughout the United States. During the 1850s, anger and fear of Germans peaked and laid the groundwork for such attitudes to prevail throughout the rest of the century. A political movement called "nativism" erupted in America. This movement favored the native-born inhabitants as opposed to immigrants. It may seem odd that this event could develop, given the fact that almost all of our citizens were related to immigrants who had originally settled this land. It is interesting that this movement simply ignored the original inhabitants of our land, the American Indian, the real native.

However, there were factors which allowed nativism to flourish. Early in the 1850s America was flooded with immigrants; most were poor Irish and Germans who had been laborers or peasants. The immigration rate from 1850 to 1855 increased five times over that of the 1840s. This inundation of immigrants strained our resources to care for them appropriately. For instance, crime costs soared and these newcomers were perceived as a threat to our social order. They crowded into our large cities and by sheer numbers and energy became a political force that could not be ignored.

The concern for social order, along with firmly held moral and religious values, led to the development of a national temperance movement during this same period. Many people felt that liquor led to personal failings and community disorder, and that abstinence from the use of alcohol was proper social policy. Most Germans opposed this temperance movement because beer drinking was a way of life with them and was the center of many of their social, cultural, and political activities.

Nativism gave rise to the development of secret societies in the early 1850s and membership in these societies was restricted to native-born Protestants. Their main goal was to reduce the potency of foreign-born political groups and alliances. These secret societies, which may have had as many as one million members at the height of their popularity, spread throughout the nation and were especially strong in the northeast. They were a force to be reckoned with, and the dominant political parties responded to them in the interest of preserving or enlarging their political bases.

These organizations came to be known as the "Know Nothings," and their political arms were named the "Order of the Star Spangled Banner" and later the "American Party." The "Know Nothings" were labeled with their strange sobriquet because "When asked what the order stood for, members answered, 'I know nothing'" (Sandburg 117-18). No member was to vote for a foreigner or a Catholic, and their slogans were "Americans must rule America" and "No papacy in the Republic" (Sandburg 118).

Out of this social and political movement came an

effort to legally proscribe the rights of foreigners. Large numbers of "Know Nothings" either gained public office or influenced public offices. In their efforts to minimize the influence of many poorly educated former laborers and peasants from Ireland and Germany, the states of Connecticut and Rhode Island imposed a literacy test. Massachusetts took a different tack when it passed a voter registration law requiring immigrants to wait two years after naturalization before becoming eligible to vote.

The "Know Nothings" were also active in the South. In 1854 a political handbill was circulated in New Orleans encouraging an anti-Catholic vote. The handbill said: ". . . the Irish are . . . making our elections scenes of violence and fraud . . . . Americans! Shall we be ruled by Irish and Germans?" (McPherson 141).

In the 1850s an old friend asked Abraham Lincoln whether he was a "Know Nothing." He replied he was not. He added he was not in favor of degrading classes of white people and that he abhorred the oppression of black people. The Declaration of Independence says that all people are created equal, and Lincoln said that by the 1850s it was being read as " . . . all men are created equal, except negroes." He added that if the "Know Nothings" gained political control the declaration would be read, " . . . all men are created equal, except negroes, and foreigners, and catholics" (Donald 189).

Thus, threads of disrespect toward Catholics, foreigners, and black men all became intertwined as we approached civil war. Germans had become characterized with some of the same non-human qualities as were ascribed to the black slave. The contribution of the Know Nothings was intensification of the hate and disrespect felt by one man toward another. Ergo, we have another element propelling us toward a cataclysmic war, and it was an underlying factor at the Nueces River as well.

The "Know Nothings" declined in popularity nearly as quickly as they had risen and were much less of a force after 1855. Part of this decline was due to the illogic and unfairness of the descendants of the original immigrants to America practicing open hostility to more recent arrivals. Additionally, the rate of immigration declined dramatically after 1854. Finally, the nation became more interested in slavery than in the newcomers and Catholicism. Before the opening of the Civil War, the "Know Nothing" movement had become split along sectional lines over the issue of slavery and was no longer a viable national force. But as far as the movement shaping attitudes and a collective psyche, the damage had been done.

In summary, there were a number of interacting factors that contributed to a climate of suspicion, anger, and hatred. In combination, these feelings promoted an atmosphere which nurtured murder. In reviewing these factors, perhaps we can gain some understanding of how our society came to accept this posture.

First, the times were violent. We were in the midst of civil war, and we were products of a violent society.

Second, slavery was an emotional issue that no longer could be approached rationally. Out of serfdom came intolerance for slavery, and out of the plantation system came a liking for that "peculiar institution." Positions were polarized and hardened.

Third, different religious views and the intertwining of religion and slavery were contributing factors.

Fourth, the two groups were of different political persuasions, with the Anglo Texan supporting the Democratic platform and the German Texan supporting the Republican platform.

Fifth, cultural factors drove the two sides apart and contributed to mutual suspicion.

Last, among Anglo Texans there probably was a xenophobic attitude in their approach to many matters relating to the German newcomers. This was coupled with a strong anti-immigrant stance that had developed in our nation.

All of these interacting factors contributed to burgeoning enmity and set the stage for death. There are lessons to be learned about the nourishment of hatred that may apply to our society and world today. Regarding the violence of the times and the violence of our society, it is well to remember that we are not born as violent people, but we learn that behavior through the process of acculturation. Society shapes our behavior. Learned behavior can be unlearned or modified. To deal with differences, it is possible to displace violence with mediation and compromise by sharpening our communicative skills, and by dedicating ourselves to resolve conflict without violence.

Americans always have had strong differences of opinion regarding social issues and justice. In the mid-nineteenth century the predominant social issue was slavery, while today the issues are more likely to be abortion or the death penalty. All these issues were, and still are, highly charged emotionally. It is wise for us to remember that in all conflicts of this nature, the issues are complex. Both sides may have valid points to support their position, but each side is prone to giving little credence to the validity of the supporting ideas on the other side. The problem is that each side is certain it is absolutely correct and that the other side is absolutely incorrect. There are no such absolutes in life. What people need to do in this situation is to listen carefully to the details of the position enunciated by the opposition, so that they might identify items on which they may be able to agree. This process of clarification may also be productive in terms of identifying positions that may be subject to modification in spite of basic disagreement. This prevents policy stagnation. As long as there is hope of movement, there is the possibility of avoiding escalation of disagreement from a verbal to an action stage.

Although we may hold different religious views, we can become more tolerant by studying the religious creeds of the other side. By understanding the difference in creeds, we may learn that there is much more we agree on than previously assumed. This may increase our level of tolerance for difference.

Even though we may disagree politically on issues, we always need to give a full hearing to the views of the other side. Frequently, a central problem is that we close ourselves off to the arguments of the other side. We may do so because of our underlying pursuit of power, ambition, and greed. These factors need to be recognized and controlled before we can really absorb what the other side is saying. This is the only way through which we may be able to reach a compromise.

We may be quite different culturally with our various customs, values, and languages, yet we still learn to live together in peace. Our nation has a fine history of being a great melting pot where diverse societies have successfully become a part of the majority group without giving up their essential distinctive features. As a consequence, these various societies have contributed much richness to the fabric of our national life. For this process to occur, it is necessary that there be good communication and goodwill between and among the different groups. Further, to promote cohesiveness, it is desirable to foster a mutual appreciation for the strengths that each entity possesses. Also, it is advantageous to break down the walls that separate us since isolation hinders the process of assimilation. That means that groups must be willing to accept some dilution of their mores to incorporate the best of other cultural groups. The key is coming to know one another and having the courage to consider different values and norms for what they may offer in terms of enriching our lives.

The unreasonable fear or hate of anything foreign or strange can best be combated through knowledge of another person as an individual and human being, who has motivations and desires similar to our own. It is necessary to avoid stereotyping, for that force hinders our ability to assess the individual as someone who has common human needs. Further, the separation of a minority group often leads to the majority dominating or attempting to control the minority. Once again, breaking down the walls that separate us is essential to gaining the understanding of one another so we can rise beyond suspicion and mistrust.

Finally, we need to recognize that a primary cause of

hatred and prejudice is ignorance. Ignorance about our fellow man arises from our lack of meaningful human contact with him. When we isolate ourselves from one another, we are sowing the seeds of prejudice, mistrust, and hatred. However, when we take the trouble to engage in meaningful dialogue with one another, there is maintained an atmosphere in which brotherhood may develop. Therefore, it is important for each of us to study one another, to interact, and to find out how we got to where we are. This is how relationships are built, and relationships are the building blocks of brotherly love. When we associate with one another in this fashion, our prejudice, bias, and hatred begin to diminish. Further, it is helpful to remind ourselves that these emotions are products of our minds, not our genes.

Human nature is not perverse—society perverts it. This being the case, it is then possible for the learned behavior of hate and prejudice to be unlearned or reversed. This is a matter of will. If we have the will, we can learn to live in peace and brotherhood.

CHAPTER 15.

THE MONUMENTS

After the affair at the Nueces River, fear of retribution by Confederate sympathizers prevented the citizens of the Hill Country from going to the site to recover bodies. They could, however, mourn the dead and remember them. They did so. The Civil War ended in April 1865, but the last battle took place on May 13, 1865, at Palmito Ranch near Brownsville, Texas.

Citizens in the Comfort area discussed how to honor their dead. It was decided that a common grave topped by a monument would suitably memorialize their sacrifice. In the summer of 1865, a delegation led by Henry Schwethelm returned to the battle site on the Nueces River. There they collected the bleached bones and returned them to Comfort for proper burial. The remains of those who died for their ideals were interred in a common grave on August 20, 1865. A monument honoring the loyalists was erected and dedicated on August 10, 1866.

On August 10, 1912, a memorial service was conducted at this monument commemorating the fiftieth anniversary of the Nueces River affair. Eight survivors were present: Jacob Gold, Peter Gold, August Hoffman, Peter Jacoby, Joseph Petsch Luckenbach, John W. Sansom, Henry Schwethelm, and Charles Vetterlein.

After more than one hundred years, this memorial began showing its age as the relentless Texas winds nearly eroded, and made illegible, the carved names on its faces.

145

The Comfort Heritage Foundation, Inc. was established in 1981 to oversee all matters relating to the *Treue der Union* Monument, and it was decided to erect a new tribute.

A magnificent new monument now exists. It is almost twenty feet high and is a native limestone structure that weighs nearly eighteen tons. It is an obelisk with four vertical name tablets. The 130th Anniversary and Rededication of the *Treue der Union* Monument took place on Monument Hill in Comfort on August 10, 1996.

This monument is the oldest Civil War monument in Texas, and the only memorial to the Union (outside of National Cemeteries) in what was Confederate territory. In 1968 it was designated as a Texas State Historical Marker, and in 1978 it was entered into the National Register of Historic Places. In 1996 the monument and adjacent gravesite were identified as State Archeological Landmarks. In 1991 the site became one of only six in the entire nation permitted by an Act of Congress to fly the U.S. Flag at half-staff in perpetuity. In addition, it is the only one of these six sites authorized to fly a period flag with thirty-six stars.[14] The Hill Country people have beautifully commemorated this important event, and the *Treue der Union* memorial does justice to these fallen idealists.

Nearly all Texans, and most people in the United States, are aware of the Alamo and the men who died there. Several hundred tourists daily make visits to the Alamo in San Antonio and pay their respects. Few Texans and other citizens of the United States are aware of the Nueces affair and the men who died there or nearby. Visits to the monument in Comfort are sparse. The Alamo story is an epic in Texas history, and deservedly so. The Nueces story is less well-known. There are similarities and differences between these two historical events.

At both the Alamo and Nueces, brave men died for their beliefs. The Alamo men were fighting because of their loyalty to the Republic of Texas. The Nueces men were fighting because of their loyalty to the United States of America. At both locations there was a pitched battle and the captured wounded were killed.

Carl Veterlein was a Unionist group member and a survivor of the Battle of the Nueces.

In this 1923 photo Henry Schwethelm (on the right) and Richard Doebbler (who drove the Model A Ford) are at the battle site.
—Private collection of Paul Burrier

The fifteenth anniversary of the Nueces "Treue der Union" Monument in Comfort, Texas (photo taken on August 10, 1881).
—Comfort Heritage Foundation, Inc. Archives

Why is the Alamo so well-known and the Nueces relatively unknown? There are several reasons. First, the Alamo battlefield is located in a large city, while the Nueces battlefield rests on private land in an isolated rural area. The Alamo memorial is located in downtown San Antonio, while the Nueces memorial is located in a small town off the interstate highway. The Alamo battlefield and monument are one and the same, while the Nueces battlefield and monument are physically separated.

Second, the Alamo is heavily publicized and a comparatively large sum of money has been expended for this purpose. There are several small examples of this publicity. The Alamo is prominently marked or discussed in four locations on the 1993 edition of the H. M. Gousha state map of Texas. On this same map the Nueces battle site is not indicated but the nearby "Alamo Village" is marked. The monument at Comfort is not indicated but the nearby "Cowboy Artists Museum" and "Bandera Downs Race Track" are marked. There is no mention of the Nueces event. On the Internet, Texas web sites prominently promote the Alamo. In contrast, there is hardly any Internet content on the Nueces affair or monument. Use of a popular web search engine ("Yahoo") reveals seven hits for "Alamo," no hits for "Nueces Massacre," and one hit for "Nueces Monument."

Third, history texts give close attention to the Alamo but not to the Nueces affair. It is to be noted that the victor of a battle or war writes the history. The Texans ultimately defeated the Mexicans at the San Jacinto river (a battle that is beautifully memorialized) and made famous the cry: "Remember the Alamo." The victorious Texans wrote the history and promoted the Alamo as the core of all things good about Texas. Had the Mexicans won and written the history, it is likely the Alamo would have been paid scant attention. The Texans defeated the Germans in the Nueces affair but have chosen to mute this history.

Fourth, a minority always has an uphill battle telling its story. The majority Anglo Texans have the advantage here over the minority German Texans. If this seems unbelievable, just ask those from the Deep South about their historical slant on the Civil War. Many of them will reply that the victorious Northern majority has written the Civil War history and that the history has never properly portrayed the Southern perspective.

The Nueces affair, and the memorial to those who did not survive this incident, deserves more recognition. So do the survivors, especially those nine men who went on to serve in the First Texas Cavalry (Union) from 1862 to 1865. All nine of them survived the war and returned to Texas. Five of them were Anglo Texans, one of whom was John Sansom, the guide. He returned home after the war and served in Ranger companies against Indians. The other four were the Anglos who joined the Nueces group on the trail on August 8. They were Howard Henderson, William Hester, Thomas J. Scott, and Warren B. Scott. The remaining four men were German Texans. They were Carl Graff, Jacob Kusenberger, Henry Schwethelm, and Adolphus Zoeller. Henry Schwethelm was one of the party who journeyed to the battle site in the summer of 1865 to recover the remains of those slain. Adolphus Zoeller was elected to the Texas Legislature after the war. While many Union sympathizers died for their beliefs in the Nueces River affair and its aftermath, and are properly revered, these nine veterans of the Union army deserve no less respect for their determination to live and to fight for their beliefs.

Restored "Treue der Union" Monument—Rededicated on August 10, 1996, the 130th anniversary of the battle.

—Photo from Comfort Heritage
Foundation, Inc. Archives
(photo by Bill Terry)

Closeup of plaque that describes the significance of this historical site.

—Author's private collection

This is the only monument to the Union, outside of National Cemeteries, in what was Confederate territory. In 1991, by an act of Congress, permission was granted to fly a period United States flag at half-staff in perpetuity.

—Private collection of Paul Burrier

The rectangle below the base of the restored monument is the original burial site of the remains of those who died for the Union cause. The site has been undisturbed since interment on August 20, 1865. A time capsule was placed within the second tier of stone above the base of the restored monument.

—Private collection of Paul Burrier

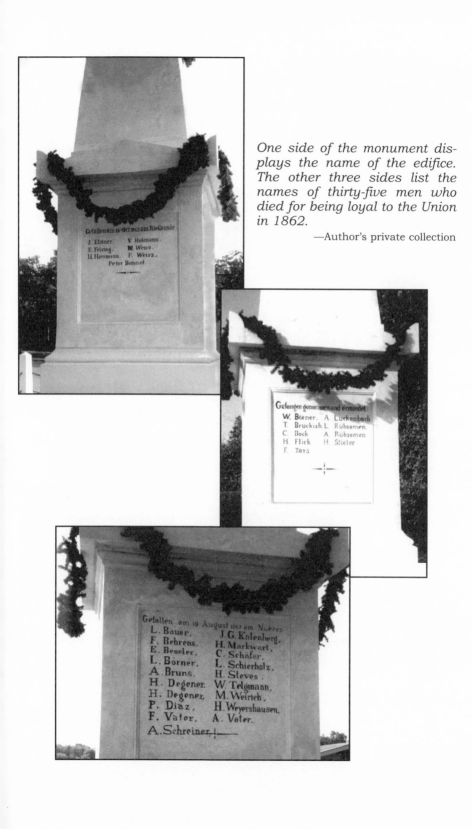

One side of the monument displays the name of the edifice. The other three sides list the names of thirty-five men who died for being loyal to the Union in 1862.

—Author's private collection

Epilogue

rom the standpoint of the majority Anglo Texans, the minority German Texans had been disloyal and sympathetic to the enemy during the Civil War. Were they ever to be trusted again? Or might they be disloyal again? Hate, fear, and mistrust, once born, die a slow death.

In 1917 the United States entered into World War I against Germany. As had been the case during the Civil War, some Germans still lived in enclaves in which little English was spoken, and they continued to isolate themselves from the larger Anglo culture. Germans once again found themselves on opposite sides of an issue of the day; they were less likely to support prohibition than other Texans. Worse, the wartime propaganda machine had cranked up, and Germans (in Europe) were branded as "vicious Huns." It was difficult for the loyal German Texans to avoid being labeled with this same epithet. Some Anglo Texans questioned the loyalty of German Texans (Hardt n.p.). "The use of the German language in public places and in schools was outlawed, and, in general, Germans were eyed with considerable distrust" (Lich 91).

Question: What impact did the incident at the Nueces River have upon attitudes toward Germans fifty-five years later?

Answer: No one knows for sure.

AFTERWORD

The role of the freethinkers in this historical episode cannot be overemphasized. Most of the men who died at the Nueces River battle, and those who were murdered after the battle, were freethinkers. The freethinkers have been described in this book, but their role needs to be reemphasized. For the men who died in the Nueces affair, being a freethinker was the *raison d'etre* of their lives—the very reason for their existence. It was this profound philosophy that caused these Germans to stand out from the others, and it strengthened their resolve to die for their beliefs.

The freethinker shunned governmental authority and control, and formed his opinions independently on the basis of reason. He rejected all forms of dogma, especially religious dogma. For the nineteenth-century German, this philosophy evolved out of his cumulative experience with serfdom, and its attendant imposition of the will of the lord upon his subjects. By 1845 the heavy hand of German government and religion caused the philosophy to foment and come to fruition in the university system. The German government attempted to repress the freethinkers, and many of them fled to Texas in order to freely exercise their beliefs.

The Texas freethinkers gathered in the Hill Country, especially in the Comfort area. There they exercised their rights to speak freely and to assemble. They also practiced their freedom from religous dogma, and they tended to be atheists. There were no churches in Comfort until 1892, and secular education was endorsed. They engaged in farming and at the same time in intellectual pursuits and the arts. Freethinkers abhorred slavery and strongly supported the United States Constitution because of its adherence to individual freedom. They believed so strongly in these things that they were willing to die for them in the Nueces affair.

In Comfort the freethinker philosophy is alive and well today. I became aware of this in August 1998 when I was there to collect artwork for this book. I was working with Gregory J. Krauter at Ingenhuett Store, and when I arrived there one early morning I mentioned that I had parked in front of the store. Since there were no markings I didn't know whether I was to park diagonally or parallel with the curb. Mr. Krauter told me that it didn't matter as long as I didn't block the street. He went on to explain that parking however you wish was one of the benefits of minimal governmental control, and that Comfort was one of the few towns in Texas which consciously chose not to be incorporated.

The freethinker philosophy is imbued in all aspects of social life as well. Later that same day two German gentlemen came to introduce themselves to me since they had heard that I was in town. Significantly, one of the gentlemen said to me, "Hello there, we are freethinkers." A brief conversation followed, and it was only later that I realized they had never given me their names. Their identification as freethinkers was more important than names.

The monument to those who died for the cause has been standing in Comfort since 1866. The community leaders are now in the process of getting a historical plaque erected to summarize the centrality of the freethinker philosophy.

Although the freethinker movement is small, it is not located only in the Comfort area. During the Civil War, Union loyalists and freethinkers were active in Austin. The Atheist Community of Austin still exists there today as a freethinker group. A similar group exists in the Dallas-Fort Worth area in Carrollton, Texas; it is identified as the North Texas Church of Freethought (A Fellowship of Unbelievers). Other groups exist elsewhere in the United States—mostly at universities. The movement is not restricted to this country. It also is found in Great Britain. *The Freethinker* is the British monthly journal for "Atheist, Secularists, Freethinkers, Rationalists, and Humanists." It is published in London, England. G. W. Foote founded *The Freethinker* in 1881.

The movement was a critical ingredient of the Union sentiment on the Nueces River. It plays an important part in community life in Comfort, Texas, today. Elsewhere it may constitute a small fringe group, but it remains active, and has been so for a century and a half.

ENDNOTES

1. This Union activity culminated in the landing of a Federal Army of seven thousand men near Brownsville, Texas, on November 6, 1863. The First Texas Cavalry (Union) consisting of 1,500 men (some of whom were German Texans from the Hill Country) captured the Confederate steamer "Mustang" and seized a Confederate barracks.

As early as July 1862 Federal cabinet members considered enrolling German Texans, who had fled to Mexico, in the Union Army. On July 11 Secretary of State Seward wrote to Secretary of War Stanton about the Germans in Matamoros, Mexico:

> . . . The condition of the loyal inhabitants of Texas in that neighborhood is represented to be so miserable, that it occurs to me those of them of a suitable age to bear arms might be most readily and effectually relieved if they would accept service in our Army. It is consequently suggested that an arrangement be made with the Secretary of the Navy for receiving any such persons on board the blockading vessel or vessels in that quarter as recruits, in order that they may be transferred to the nearest United States military command (OR Ser. 1, Vol. 9, 684).

Also, President Lincoln was interested in establishing a Federal presence in Texas to discourage the increasing French imperialistic presence in Mexico. During the Civil War, France sent 35,000 troops to Mexico and installed Maximillian as Emperor.

Additionally, Texans were transporting cotton across the Rio Grande to Mexican ports where it was shipped to English and European ports in exchange for merchandise and army supplies. The usual cotton movement from East Texas was by wagon train to Brownsville, and from there across the Rio Grande to Matamoros. At Matamoros, the cotton was loaded on river steamers and taken to the village of Bagdad where it was loaded on ocean-going vessels. Bagdad was a sleepy village, but it had the advantage of being in a neutral nation, not subject to the Union naval blockade, and had deep water outside an offshore sandbar. The village became a thriving cotton market where one could always find bales of cotton awaiting loading. The Union hoped to stop this traffic by strengthening the naval blockade along the Texas coast and moving troops inland from Brownsville to Laredo and Eagle Pass on the Rio Grande (and not far from the Nueces River affair). They were partially successful. The cotton trail then moved up to Eagle Pass making the trip to the ocean more difficult for the Texans.

2. Edwin Clark, who became governor on March 16, 1861, was the first of the Confederate governors in Texas. Clark had been Governor Sam Houston's lieutenant governor, and replaced him when Houston was deposed because of his opposition to secession. Francis Lubbock, who was installed in office on November 7, 1861, followed him. Pendleton Murrah succeeded Lubbock, in turn, on November 5, 1863.

3. The selected campsite was located about twenty miles southwest of Fort Wood, an abandoned Federal facility that housed Confederate troops. One Confederate soldier stationed there on June 15, 1861, was W. W. Heartsill and he describes that area in his diary. He says, "The waters of this strange, beautiful [Nueces] river are so transparent that I can see the bottom. I can see the small pebbles on the bottom at a depth of thirty feet, . . . but farther downstream I can walk on dry sand and rocks all the way across the stream. The waters . . . are cold and pleasant to drink while their beauty adds to the grandeur of the country which surrounds the post. The valleys and plains are covered with luxurious grasses and pecan trees, while chapparal, Spanish persimmons, and wild plums are scattered about the countryside" (Heartsill 106).

4. The German influence on elections was being felt nationally. In May 1859, in the midst of his quest for the presidency, Lincoln actively tried to move the German American voter away from the Democratic Party toward the Republican Party. He did so by secretly buying, for $400, the weekly German-language newspaper *Illinois Staats-Anzeiger* of Springfield, Illinois. Under Lincoln's direction, the editor was to continue publishing a Republican paper in German with occasional articles in English. In the election of 1860 Lincoln received only four percent of the popular vote in Southern states, mostly from anti-slavery Germans in St. Louis and vicinity. The proportion of German Americans voting Republican in the nation in 1860 was less than half. However, the defections from the Democratic Party were dramatic and may have helped provide the margin of Republican victory in Pennsylvania, Indiana, and Illinois. (For discussions of the German American vote see *Lincoln* by David Herbert Donald [242], *Abraham Lincoln* by Carl Sandburg [155], and Battle Cry of Freedom by James M. McPherson [233 and footnote 41]).

5. Of particular help here have been the unpublished manuscripts of Col. Wm. Paul Burrier Sr. (P. O. Box 1084, Leakey Texas 78873-7084) entitled "The Myths," "Notes," and "Bios," pamphlets from the Comfort (Texas) Heritage Foundation and the Comfort (Texas) Chamber of Commerce; the unpublished work of Kenn Knopp (407 N.

Cora Strasse, Fredericksburg TX 78682-4213, email: kenknopp @ktc.com) entitled "The Fredericksburg Texas Manuscripts," undated; and Chapter VI, "Comfort During the Civil War," found in the Ransleben book cited elsewhere.

It should be noted that various authorities disagree on exactly how many men died and where those who are listed here died. That is particularly true of those who are listed as being killed immediately after the battle on August 10, 1862. These inconsistencies probably are due to the fact that the bones of the bodies were collected three years after this incident, and also that memory may have faded because some accounts were written many years after the affair. Additionally some survivor's accounts probably exaggerated casualty figures in order to prove a point or to fix blame. However, there is little doubt that all the listed men were in fact in the Nueces River affair and died for their beliefs.

6. Fritz Lange is honored as one of those who died at the Rio Grande but his name has not been placed on the *Treue der Union* monument. A local historian, Gregory J. Krauter, told this author on July 18, 1998, that Lange's involvement was not verified until many years after his death and consequently his name never appeared on the original monument. According to Mr. Krauter, Fritz Lange's name does not appear on the restored monument at the request of a state agency, which desired that historical integrity be preserved and the name not added.

7. This locale came to be known as "Dead Men's Hole." Although unconfirmed by me personally, the bodies of Henderson, Tegener, Scott, and Nelson are supposedly buried at the Spring Creek Cemetery, on the west side of Spring Creek and the north side of Old Harper Road just west of its eastern junction with US 290.

8. The .52-caliber Sharps carbine and rifle was an excellent weapon that was patented in 1848 by Christian Sharps and was the first successful breech-loader. Before the Civil War, Southern states purchased the carbine for use by state cavalry units, particularly those on the frontier who were dealing with the Indian problem. During his 1854 journey through Texas, Frederick Olmsted carried the Sharps rifle and thought highly of it. During the war 5,000 copies of the weapon were manufactured at Richmond.

John Brown used the Sharps rifle on his raid at Harper's Ferry where he seized the U.S. Armory in preparation for an uprising by the slaves. This made the Sharps rifle famous and thereafter it was nicknamed "Beecher's Bible." This was in reference to Harriet Beecher Stowe who, in 1852, had published *Uncle Tom's Cabin*, which inflamed the people of the North against slavery. Her father was a renowned preacher, thus the sobriquet. It is ironic that this Cavalry unit used "Beecher's Bible" in the effort to preserve slavery.

9. Benjamin became attorney general, then secretary of war, and

finally secretary of state for the Confederacy. He was the first Jew to become an U.S. senator, and while serving there he entered into a life-long friendship with Jefferson Davis. He was said to be one of the best lawyers in the South and frequently he was referred to as the "brains of the Confederacy."

10. This is the same Henry Heth who, on June 30, 1863, said to Gen. A. P. Hill, "'If there is no objection, I will take my division tomorrow and go to Gettysburg and get those shoes.'" "'None in the world.' Hill told him" (Foote, 465).

11. The Fredericksburg-Comanche Peace Treaty of 1847 is memorable in that it is thought to be the only treaty with Native-Americans that was honored by both sides.

12. Interestingly, a number of historians believe that the type of government organization had a lot to do with the outcome of the Civil War. The Union, with its strong central government, was able to effectively marshal its abundant resources. The CSA, with its more decentralized government, which placed emphasis upon the rights of individual states, had more difficulty organizing and marshalling its meager resources. This problem was particularly dramatic when a state governor would veto a CSA plan to use his state's troops in another state.

13. Today some German communities set aside special times for German-speaking activities. For example, the German-Texan Heritage Society promotes a German *Stammtisch* (speak German only day) on each Thursday from 12:00 P.M. to 1:00 P.M. The format is casual and you are told to bring your brown bag lunch if you desire. At the University of Texas Department of Germanic Languages, a daily luncheon *Stammtisch* is held so students may practice their German.

14. It is interesting that the thirty-six star flag should be chosen. The official United States flag on August 10, 1862, was the thirty-four star flag. It had been adopted when Kansas was admitted as a State on January 29, 1861. The thirty-five star flag was approved after West Virginia was admitted as a state on June 19, 1863, and the thirty-six star flag was chosen after Nevada was admitted as a state on October 31, 1864. The thirty-six star flag was chosen to fly at Comfort because it was this nation's flag when the *Treue der Union* monument was dedicated on August 10, 1866.

WORKS CITED

Biesele, Rudolph L. *The History of German Settlements in Texas 1831-1861*. Austin: German-American Heritage Society, 1987.

Boatner III, Mark M. *The Civil War Dictionary* (Revised Edition). New York: Vintage Books, 1991.

Buenger, Walter L. "Texas and the Riddle of Secession." *Lone Star Blue and Gray: Essays on Texas in the Civil War*. Ed. Ralph A. Wooster. Austin: Texas State Historical Association, 1995. 1-26.

Burrier, Wm. Paul. "The Myths" ms., 1 June 1997, 1-27

—-."Notes" ms., n.d., 22-31.

—-."Bios" ms., n.d., n. pag.

Catton, Bruce. *The Coming Fury*. Garden City, New York: Doubleday & Company, Inc., 1961.

Chesebrough, David B. (Ed.) *God Ordained This War*. Columbia, S.C.: University of South Carolina Press, 1991.

Cramer, Ernest. "My Beloved Parents:" Unpublished letter, October 30, 1862, n. pag.

Donald, David Herbert. *Lincoln*. New York: Simon & Schuster (Touchstone), 1996.

Elliott, Claude. "Union Sentiment in Texas, 1861-1865." *Lone Star Blue and Gray: Essays on Texas in the Civil War*. Ed. Ralph A. Wooster. Austin: Texas State Historical Association, 1995. 81-107.

Engels, Frederick. *The Peasant War in Germany*. Trans. Moissaye J. Olgin. Transcribed by zodiac@interlog.com in July 1995. Online 4 January 1996. Internet. 9 July 1977. Available http://csf.colorado.edu/psn/marx/Archive/1850-PWG.

Foote, Shelby. *The Civil War: A Narrative. Volume 2, Fredericksburg to Meridian*. New York: Vintage Books, 1963.

Fremantle, A.J.L. "Three Months in the Southern States: April-June, 1863." 1864. *Texas, The Dark Corner of the Confederacy: Contemporary Accounts of the Lone Star State*. Ed. B. P. Gallaway. 3rd ed. Lincoln: University of Nebraska Press, 1994. 149-52.

Gallaway, B. P., Ed. *Texas, The Dark Corner of the Confederacy: Contemporary Accounts of the Lone Star State*. 3rd ed. Lincoln: University of Nebraska Press, 1994.

Haley, James L. *Texas: An Album of History.* Garden City, N.Y.: Doubleday, 1985.

Hardt, Bill. "Anglo-Texan and German-Texan Friction During World War I." *Armadillo.* A Shared Past, Chapter 19 (1994): n. pag. Online. Internet. 14 July 1997. Available http://riceinfo.rice.edu/armadillo/texas/sharedpast/german.html.

Heartsill, W. W. "Fourteen Hundred and 91 Days in the Confederate Army; or Camp Life, Day by Day of the W. P. Lane Rangers from April 19, 1861 to May 20, 1865." 1876. Facsimile reprint. Ed. Bell I. Wiley. *Texas, the Dark Corner of the Confederacy: Contemporary Accounts of the Lone Star State.* Ed. B. P. Gallaway. 3rd ed. Lincoln: University of Nebraska Press, 1994. 94-107.

Heidler, Jeanne T. "Embarrassing Situation: David E. Twiggs and the Surrender of United States Forces in Texas, 1861." *Lone Star Blue and Gray: Essays on Texas in the Civil War.* Ed. Ralph A. Wooster. Austin: Texas State Historical Association, 1995. 29-44.

Hoffman, August. "The Blackest Crime in Texas Warfare." *Dallas Morning News* May 5, 1929, n. pag.

—. Untitled Letter, September 1, 1925, n. pag.

Kuechler, Jacob. Untitled letter. n.d. n. pag.

Lich, Glen E. *The German Texans.* Rev. ed. San Antonio: The University of Texas Institute of Texan Cultures at San Antonio. 1996.

McPherson, James M. *Battle Cry of Freedom: The Civil War Era.* New York: Ballantine Books, 1988.

Michener, James A. *Texas.* New York: Fawcett Crest, 1985.

OR Abbr. "Official Records of the Union and Confederate Armies" *The Civil War CD- ROM: The War of the Rebellion.* CD-ROM v.1.0. Carmel, Indiana: Guild Press of Indiana, Inc., 1996.

Olmsted, Frederick Law. *A Journey Through Texas.* 1857. Austin, Texas: University of Texas Press, 1978.

Ransleben, Guido E. *A Hundred Years of Comfort in Texas.* San Antonio: The Naylor Company, 1954.

Sanchez, Mario L. "Secession and Civil War." *Armadillo.* A Shared Experience, Part II, Historical Survey (1994): n. pag. Online. Internet. 14 July, 1997. Available http://riceinfo.rice.edu/armadillo/past/book/part2/civilwar.html.

Sandburg, Carl. *Abraham Lincoln: The Prairie Years and The War Years.* One Volume Ed. New York: Harcourt, Brace & World, Inc., 1954.

Sansom, John W. "Account Book," 1911: 29.

—. *Battle of Nueces River in Kinney County, Texas, August 10th, 1862.* San Antonio, Texas: n.p., 1905.

—. Letter to James T. DeShields, August 14, 1907. n. pag.

—. "The German Citizens were Loyal to the Union." *Hunter's Magazine*, November, 1911, Vol. II, No. 1: 12

—-. "Memoirs of Capt. John W. Sansom, 1834-1916." ms, n.d. n.p. n. pag.

Schwethelm, Heinrich Joseph. "I was a Survivor of the Nueces Battle." (As told to Albert Schutze). "San Antonio Press," (Frontier Times Section), August 31, 1924.

Selcer, Richard and Burrier, William Paul. "What Really Happened on the Nueces River?" *North & South.* January 1998: 56-67.

Vasile, Michael A. "Guerrilla Warfare in the American Civil War." Online. Internet. Available http://www.lsu.edu/other/other/acwguer.html. 30 April 1997.

Wakelyn, Jon L. *Biographical Dictionary of the Confederacy.* Westport, Connecticut: Greenwood Press, 1977.

Weber, Adolf Paul. *The German Pioneer: The Story of the Germans in Texas.* San Antonio, Texas: Self-Published, 1894.

INDEX

Brownsville, 17, 18, 38, 40, 145, 155
Bruns, Albert, 76
Bruckish, Theodore, 81
Brunswich, Germany, 71
Buegel, John T., 19
Burgmann (Bergmann), Charles, 43
"Bushwhackers," 41, 79, 81, 82, 84, 90, 91, 92
"Butcher of Fredericksburg," 40

C

Caldwell County, 89
California, 13, 17
Camp Verde, 38
Carlshaven, 61, 62
Carrizo, 17
Castro's Colony, 57
Castroville, 79, 93
Cedar-Brake, 10, 44, 78
Charlemagne, 49
Charleston, South Carolina, 17, 38
Charlettenberg, Germany, 90
Church
    Baptist, 130, 131, 133
    Catholic, 51, 52, 56, 132, 133, 139, 140
    Episcopal, 131, 132
    Lutheran, 52, 69, 132, 133
    Methodist, 130, 131, 133
    of England 130
Cibolo Creek, 79
Clareno Ranch, 18
Clark (Edward, and Proclamation), 23, 156
Clark, Walter Van Tilburg, 124
Colorado, 17
Colorado River, 56, 61
Comal Springs, 56
Comfort, 4, 8, 21, 25, 27, 38, 61, 67-69, 76, 79, 81-84, 87, 90, 97, 131, 133, 137, 145, 146, 149, 156, 157, 160

Comfort Heritage Foundation, 146, 156
Comfort Militia, Precinct #2, 27
Communist, 60, 67, 131
Compromise of 1850, 13
Compromise of 1820, (Missouri Compromise) 13, 127
Confederate
    Military, 37, 78, 87, 94, 100, 105, 116
    Miscellaneous, 10, 11, 17, 18, 19, 20, 21, 23, 24, 27, 33, 35, 36, 37, 39, 40, 41, 44, 45, 46, 66, 77, 78, 79, 81, 87, 89, 90, 91, 92, 93, 94, 100, 102, 103, 105, 106, 108, 109, 112, 113, 114, 115, 116, 117, 118, 119, 121, 122, 128, 132, 145, 146
Confederate States of America (CSA), 3, 9, 14, 21, 24
    Confederation, 3, 52, 53, 54, 128, 134
    Congress, 12, 14, 17, 23, 36, 53, 56, 106, 107, 108, 122, 134, 146
    Conscription Act, 93
    District Court, 78
    Military Commission, 78, 87, 94, 98, 100, 108
Congress of Vienna, 53
Constitution
    Confederate, 24
    General, 59, 126
    Mexican, 56
    Texas, 57
    United States, 54, 67, 107, 126, 134, 135
Copperhead, 22
Cortina, Juan, 17, 18
Cotton, 12, 13, 18, 38, 41, 60, 129, 155
Cramer, Ernest, 8, 25, 36, 39, 71, 78, 83, 84
Curry's Creek, 9

Know-Nothings, 139-140
Kuechler, Jacob, 8, 27, 29, 37,
    39, 45, 66, 71, 77, 83, 89,
    91
Kusenberger, Jacob, 84, 150
Kyle, Jack, 94

L

Lange, Fritz, 90, 157
Laredo, 156
Latin language, 68, 133, 136,
    137
Latin settlements, 68, 137
Laurel Creek, Madison County,
    North Carolina, 114, 115
Lee, A. T., 36
Lee, Robert E., 17, 113
Lichtenau, Silesia, Germany, 47
Lieber, Francis, 117
Lilly, Edwin, 44, 78
Lincoln, Abraham, 12, 13, 14,
    18, 21, 25, 106, 107, 113,
    116, 135, 140, 155, 156
Live Oak Creek, 66, 77
Llano River, 60
Lone Star Republic, 57
Loyalty Oath
    Confederate, 3, 24, 41, 107,
        108, 121
    Union, 107
Lubbock, Francis, 38, 104, 156
Luckenbach, August, 81
Luckenbach Bushwhackers, 41,
    79, 81, 82, 84, 90, 91, 92
Luckenbach, Joseph Petsch,
    145
Luther, Martin, 50, 132
"Lynch Law," 41, 123

M

McCulloch, H. E., 24, 33
McRae, Colin D., 11, 39, 43-44,
    46, 77, 78, 83, 98-101, 120
Markwort, Heinrich, 76
Marschall, William, 47

Marshall, North Carolina, 113-
    116
martial law, 25, 34, 35, 37, 39,
    40, 78, 91, 93, 104-107,
    122
Marx, Karl, 61, 67
massacre, 82, 94, 98, 99, 100,
    102, 103, 149
Matamoros, Mexico, 10, 18, 85,
    155
Medina River, 63, 81
Medio Creek, 81
Meusebach, John O., 64-65, 67
Mexican War, 13, 20, 35, 38, 58,
    97, 124
Mid-German Uplands, 48
Minnesota, 58
Mississippi, 12, 15, 27, 104,
    106, 129
Molzberger, Auguste, 84
Monument, 145-146, 149, 157
Moore's Mill, Missouri, 27
Murrah, Pendleton, 156
"Mustang," 155

N

Nacogdoches, 56
Napoleon, 53, 126
Nashville, Tennessee, 27
Nassau, Duchy of, 77, 81, 82,
    84, 90
Nassau Farm, 61
National Register of Historic
    Places, 146
nativism, 123, 137, 138, 139
Nebraska, 13, 127
Nelson, Hiram, 92
Nevada, 17, 158
New Braunfels, 56, 61, 62, 63,
    65, 66, 69, 80
New Mexico, 13, 17, 20, 27,
    38
New Orleans, Louisiana, 4, 10,
    18, 27, 48, 85, 140
Nolan, Matthew, 18